THE ADVENTURES OF
A FORTY-NINER

The Adventures of
A Forty-Miner

By Daniel Knower, With an Introduction
& Extended Notes by Kenneth M. Johnson.

———

Lewis Osborne : Ashland, 1971

INTRODUCTION

DANIEL KNOWER, member of a prominent and respected mid-state New York family, was a dentist by profession, a speculator by avocation. He was born in 1823 at Albany and may have lived for a time at Knowersville, a community which flourished in that region in the 1850s.

Late in 1848, when he was 25 years old, Dr. Knower organized and invested in the outfitting of a party of Albany gold-seekers who sailed for California in January, 1849. Shortly thereafter, becoming doubtful of the success of this venture, he conceived a second enterprise, that of building dwelling-houses in the East and shipping them in sections around the Horn to capitalize on the housing shortage in San Francisco where lumber prices were exorbitant. He had twelve of the buildings constructed that spring, arranged for their transportation on the packet-ship *Prince de Joinville* in June, and took passage himself on the steamer *Crescent City* from New York on July 1, 1849.

Traveling by the Panama Isthmus route, Knower arrived at San Francisco in early September. He quickly became engaged in a wide range of investments and transactions—from blankets to sailing-ships—and did not return to the East until a year later. His California experience appears to have been the great adventure of his life, for afterward he settled down to practice his profession at Schoharie, a county-seat west of Albany, New York, where he married Rugene Charlotte Lavina Georgianna Michaels in 1853 and became active in local civic affairs. He was a member of The Society of California Pioneers, an affiliation in which he took great pride, and he followed its activities closely. He died in 1897 at Schoharie.

Knower carried to California two letters of introduction from William L. Marcy (a distant relative): one to Colonel Jonathan D. Stevenson and one to General Persifor F. Smith. These letters certainly carried weight, because Marcy was a most important man of the time, a lawyer and statesman who had an imposing record of public service. He served three terms as governor of

New York, had been a United States Senator for New York, secretary of war under President Polk, and was later to be secretary of state under President Pierce. Knower never delivered his letter to General Smith, as the latter was then away from San Francisco. But Marcy's letter introducing Knower to Colonel Stevenson appears to have been quite helpful.

Colonel Stevenson had been commissioned to form what was known as The First New York Volunteers, later simply "Stevenson's Regiment," to sail around the Horn to California. The first mission of the regiment was to augment the military forces engaged in the war with Mexico; the second was to place in California a substantial American population which it was hoped would stay there and develop the interests of the United States. The first mission proved to be unnecessary, for by the time the troops reached California in March, 1847, the fighting was over; however, many, including Stevenson himself, did remain in California.

Stevenson, with whom Knower was to have various business associations, had been a colonel in the New York State Militia and was an ex-state-senator as well. He led an active and successful business life in San Francisco as a merchant and real estate promoter. The city of Pittsburg, California is the result of his grand scheme to create a "New York of the Pacific" which he hoped would supplant San Francisco as the major port of the west coast. Stevenson was honest, able and well-liked. He was the first Grand Master of Free Masons in the state.

Knower's *Adventures of a Forty-Niner,* first published in 1894, has a definite and secure place among the annals of the gold rush period. Robert Ernest Cowen, eminent bibliographer of California history, in his fine *A Bibliography of the History of California and the Pacific Coast,* 1510–1906 (San Francisco, 1914) notes that although "Numerous inaccuracies in the spelling of proper names have somewhat disfigured this work . . . the story of this wholesome old Argonaut has not suffered, nor is its interest lessened."

10

To a degree, Knower might be said to be to California history as Grandma Moses is to New England folk-art. Both, late in life, felt an urge for creative expression; both were clearly non-professionals, but with simplicity and honesty both have produced works of charm and interest. Knower's memoir is of particular value in that it covers business life in San Francisco during the important period of 1849–'50. Commercial activities were then of course very different from those elsewhere in the United States. Fortunes were quickly made and as quickly lost; conditions were chaotic, and feast or famine was the rule. Of all of this, Knower was a part, and in the main it is what the book is about. While he made two trips to the northern mines, he was not primarily a miner and his principal interests were in trade and commerce. We thus see the gold rush through the eyes of a merchant rather than those of a miner.

The account is also important as one of the very few which deal extensively with commercial affairs in San Francisco at this time. There are literally hundreds of books on the trip to California and life in the mines; but those concerned in the main with business life can be counted on the fingers of one hand. The first in this group that comes to mind is *Seventy-Five Years in California* by William Heath Davis (San Francisco, 1970). Davis came to the Golden State in 1838, and from 1845 on was a resident of San Francisco, a merchant, ship owner and a prominent citizen. His book is truly great, but it covers activities prior to 1849 in much more detail than thereafter; it also covers many matters other than business. All of the standard histories of California (notably Bancroft and Hittell) treat of commerce, but those of course were not written by participants.

Next to be considered is *A Yankee Trader in the Gold Rush; The Letters of Franklin A. Buck* (Boston, 1930). The *Letters* range from 1846 to 1881 and all are of interest since Buck was a competent observer and reporter. He arrived in San Francisco on August 6, 1849 with a mixed cargo of goods after an around-the-Horn voyage. Thereafter he did about everything: had stores at Sacramento and Weaverville, speculated in flour, operated a sawmill, mined, and raised hogs. Buck made an extensive voyage to Hawaii and Tahiti and returned to San Francisco to join the rush to the silver mines of the Comstock Lode in 1869. While his letters cover a great deal more than the economics of trade, they are nevertheless a valuable contribution to the *genre* of the literature of commerce.

In 1956, the Huntington Library at San Marino published *California Gold Rush Merchant—The Journal of Stephen Chapin Davis* (edited by Benjamin B. Richards). Although this has a good many skips, it is a day-by-day journal of events recorded at the time of their happening. The author arrived at San Francisco on September 4, 1850, by way of Panama. He and his brother Josiah operated a store and a miners' boarding-house very successfully at Long Bar on the Yuba River. Stephen returned to New York in the latter part of 1851, but was back in San Francisco in April, 1852, again *via* Panama. In partnership with a J. Hilliard of Nashua, New Hampshire (Stephen's home town), he had a store at Coulterville for about two years, and in 1854 returned by the Panama route to Nashua. This book is splendid source material on the logistics of supplying miners in goldfields.

Josiah Belden—1841, California Overland Pioneer: His Memoir and Early Letters (Georgetown, 1962), is largely based on a statement Belden gave to one of the assistants of Hubert Howe Bancroft. Belden worked as a clerk for Thomas O. Larkin at Monterey, and operated a branch store for him at Santa Cruz; later he had his own prosperous establishment at San Jose, and became a man of substantial means.

And that is about the extent of the commerce-oriented, participant-reported literature of this period. Most merchants were too busy to write memoirs or failed to realize that what they were doing would later be of special interest.

Many works on the 1849–'50 period, of course, contain passing references to business conditions and transactions. Perhaps the most important of these is *The Larkin Papers* published in ten volumes by the University of California Press at Berkeley. Thomas O. Larkin, U. S. Consul, merchant and trader at Monterey, played a most significant part in the early history of California; his involvement included mercantile, military, political and social affairs. His story is well told in *From Cowhides to Golden Fleece* (Stanford, 1939), by Reuben L. Underhill. Another source on Larkin is *First and Last Consul—A Selection of Letters* (Palo Alto, 1970), edited by John A. Hawgood.

One of the more interesting subjects of Knower's *Adventures* is his account of the importation of pre-fabricated houses. While quite a few businessmen brought such buildings to San Francisco, research has failed to locate any other statement by anyone who did this. In *Men and Memories of San Francisco in the Spring of '50* by T. A. Barry and B. A. Patten (San Francisco, 1872), there is the following report:

"The ship *Oxnard,* Captain Cole, arrived in San Francisco, November 22, 1849 bringing twenty-five wooden houses, all numbered in sections, and fitted in Boston for erection in San Francisco. Charles R. Bond brought them out for Wm. D. M. Howard, who retained twelve of them, after selling twelve to Captain J. L. Folsom, and one to Captain Cole.

"Three or four of them were erected on Mission Street, near Third, Messrs. Howard, Mellus and Brannan occupying three of them. Captain Folsom erected others on Mission, between First and Second streets; on Minna, Natoma, Tehama and Folsom streets."

These houses were well made, and were excellent examples of good New England craftsmanship. In San Francisco, one still survives in 1971 and in San Jose several were standing until the middle part of this century.

The Adventures of a Forty-Niner was obviously privately printed. While the exact quantity of the edition is not known, it was probably only 500 or a thousand copies. Curiously, the title on the spine of the original volume is *The Days of the Forty-Niners,* while the title-page has "The Adventures . . .". For its time, the book is an example of good bookmaking: the paper is laid and the printing clear and even, the binding is gold-stamped cloth over boards.

As Cowan has noted, Knower mis-spelled a good many proper names in his manuscript. For example, Macondray appears in the original as "McCondery," and Realejo is "Relago." There seemed to be no point in retaining Knower's spelling for the sake of quaintness at the expense of accuracy, so names (and a few place-location errors) have been corrected; otherwise the text is exactly as the author wrote it. Knower also had a habit of referring to persons by a single initial, *e.g.,* "Mr. K." or "Colonel M." To the extent that it was possible, these have been identified in the Notes herein; sometimes there was no clue, or only an educated guess could be made, and where this was the case it is so indicated.

While the narrative was composed many years after the events described, Knower apparently retained some good memoranda, and his work appears quite accurate as to matters in which he personally participated, but he was not overly cautious about information received from others. There is thus some occasional misinformation in the text, and where it was detected, this also is suggested in the Notes.

—Kenneth M. Johnson

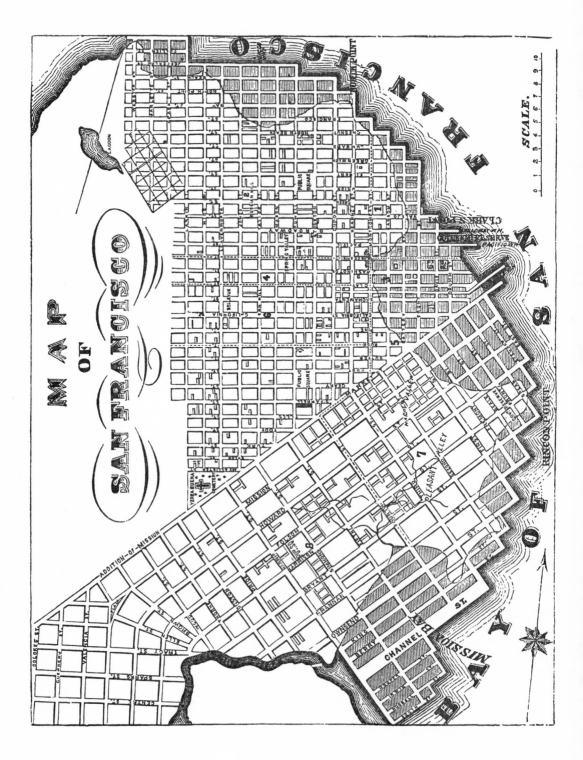

PREFACE

THE DISCOVERY of gold in California, in 1848, with its other mineral resources, including the Almaden quicksilver mine at San José, which is an article of first necessity in working gold or silver ore; and the great silver mines of Nevada, in 1860, the Comstock lode, in which, in ten years, from five to eight hundred millions of gold and silver were taken out, a larger amount than was ever taken from one locality before, the Almaden quicksilver mine being the second most productive of any in the world, the one in Spain being the largest, said to be owned by the Rothschilds. Its effect upon the general prosperity and development of our country has been immense, almost incalculable. Before these discoveries the amount of gold in the United States was estimated at about seventy millions, now it is conceded to be seven hundred millions. The Northern Pacific coast was then almost unpopulated. California a territory three times as large as New York and Oregon and the State of Washington, all now being cultivated and containing large and populous cities, and railroads connecting them with the East. Why that country should have remained uninhabited for untold ages, where universal stillness must have prevailed as far as human activity is concerned, is one of the unfathomable mysteries of nature. It is only one hundred and twenty-five years since the Bay of San Francisco was first discovered, one of the grandest harbors in the world, being land-locked, extending thirty miles, where all the vessels of the world could anchor in safety. The early pioneers of those two years immediately after the gold was discovered (of which I am writing) are passing away. As Ossian says, "People are like the waves of the ocean, like the leafs of woody marvin that pass away in the rustling blast, and other leaves lift up their green heads." There is probably not five per cent of the population of California to-day, of those days, scenes and events of which I have tried to portray. Another generation have taken their places who can know but little of those times except by tradition. I, being one of the pioneers, felt it a duty, or an in-

17

spiration seemed to come over me as an obligation I owed to myself and compatriots of those times, to do what I could to perpetuate the memory of them to some extent in the history of our country as far as I had the ability to do it.

—THE AUTHOR

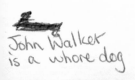

ADVENTURES OF A FORTY-NINER.

THE WRITER was practising his profession in the city of Albany, his native place, in 1848, when reports came of the discovery of gold in California. In a short time samples of scales of the metal of the river diggings were on exhibition, sent to friends in the city in letters. Many of Colonel Stevenson's regiment had been recruited in that city. Soon these rumors were exaggerated. It was said that barrels of gold were dug by individuals named. Soon the excitement extended all over the country, and the only barrier to wealth, it seemed, was the difficulty of getting to the Eldorado. Why the discovery of gold there should have produced so much excitement cannot be fathomed. It seemed an era in human affairs, like the Crusades and other events of great importance that occur. Your correspondent became one of its votaries, and organized a company to go to the gold rivers and secure a fortune for all interested in it, and it seemed all that was required was to get there and return in a short time and ride in your carriage and astonish your friends with your riches. Suffice it to say, this company was fully organized (with its by-laws and system of government drawn up by the writer), and sailed from the port of New York on the ship *Tarrolinta* on the 13th of January, 1849, to go around Cape Horn, arriving in San Francisco on the following July. From that time I became absorbed in all the news from the gold regions, and losing confidence somewhat in the certainty of a fortune from my interest in the company, and reading of the high price of lumber, the scarcity of houses, and the extraordinary high wages of mechanics there, conceived the project of shipping the materials for some houses there, having all the work put on them here that could be done, thus saving the difference in wages, and to have them arrive there before the rainy season set in, and thus realize the imaginary fortune that I had expected from my interest in the company. In the following spring I had twelve houses constructed. The main point upon which my speculation seemed to rest was to get them to San Francisco before the rainy reason commenced. I went to New York to secure freight for them in the fastest vessel. Fortunately for me, as I conceived at the time, I found the day before I arrived in New York, the *Prince de Joinville,* a Havre packet ship, had been put up to sail for the port of San Francisco, and as yet had engaged no freight. I made a bargain with them at once to take my houses at sixty cents per square foot, and had the contract signed, half to be delivered at the side of the ship by such a date and the other half at a subsequent date. I delivered the first half of the houses on the time agreed, sending them down the Hudson river by a barge on a tow. I sent the second half on a barge to get there on the day they were due, apprehending no trouble, I going down myself a few days in advance. They commenced complaining at the ship that they would not have room for the balance of my houses on board, although I had their written contract to take them at sixty cents per foot.

There was great California excitement about this time, and other parties had come to the conclusion that the *Prince de Joinville* was probably the fastest ship taking freight for San Francisco. I saw them accept offers at $1.50 per foot, when their contract with me was for less than half that price, which would make a difference of several thousand dollars in their favor. So, if the balance of my houses did not arrive within the time stated in the contract, they would not be taken on that vessel, and my speculation ruined. The time was up the next day at twelve o'clock. I was down on the Battery the next morning early watching for the tow, with the barge with my houses. The ship was at the dock in the East river. About ten o'clock, A. M., I had the good fortune to see the barge rounding the Battery. I cried out to the captain to cut loose from the tow, employ the first steam tug and I would pay the bill, which he did, getting on the side of the vessel by eleven o'clock, thus saving my contract by one hour. But they did not commence taking them on board, so the captain of the barge put a demurrage of $20 per day for detention. In the meantime, I had bought my ticket to sail by the steamer *Georgia* to the Isthmus to go on the 1st of July which was but a few days off.[1] They, seeing that I had them on my contract, came to me and said that my houses should go on their ship according to contract, if they had to throw other freight out, and that they would sign a regular bill of lading for all the material deliverable to me upon the arrival of the *Prince de Joinville* at the port of San Francisco, and take my carpenters' specifications for the description of them, which seemed all right to me.

The following is an article from the *Albany Evening Atlas* of June 23, 1849:

"CALIFORNIA HOUSES.

"Our estimable fellow citizen Dr. Knower, who is to start for California by the Crescent City *via* Panama, is about to ship to that place twelve houses, complete and ready to put up on arrival at San Francisco. The venture is a costly one, the freight on the material approaching the cost of as many frame buildings in this quarter, and the projector, we think, has managed the speculation with great foresight and judgment. The best timber has been selected, and the best workmen employed, and a plan of architecture pursued, which is supposed to offer the greatest advantages with the most economical expenditures of material. Four of these buildings are 18 feet front and 25 feet deep. A partition running lengthways divides the buildings into two rooms, and the stairs leads to a second platform, which is large enough for bedrooms, or for storing materials and tools of miners. Two others are 18 feet front and 18 feet deep, with a small extension in the rear of 8 feet. Two are 16 feet in front and 22 feet deep, with the entrance on the gable front; and the others are 18 feet front by 14 deep. The sides of the building will be composed of a double framework of boards planed, grooved and tongued, fitting air tight on each side of the timber, the interval between them being either filled with the moss of the country or left vacant, the confined column of the air being found sufficient to keep off the excess of cold or heat. The roofs of all the buildings shed from the front, except two of which are of gable shape. The roofs are to be made of solid, close-fitting planks, covered with fine ticking and coated with the patent indestructible fire-proof paint, and applications which our citizens have just begun to use here, and which they have found entirely successful.

"The houses can be easily transported to the placers or may be put up on the sea-board. We should suppose that the numerous land-owners who are speculating on the prospects of future cities would be glad to give the land necessary for the location of this village.

"The houses go by the *Prince de Joinville,* a first-class vessel, which leaves New York soon."

I SAILED ON THE steamer which left New York at 5 P. M., July 1, 1849. Friends were there to see me off, but there were no persons on the boat that I had ever seen before—I was wondering who would be my first acquaintance. Being very tired, I retired soon to my berth, and woke up the next morning on the broad ocean. Two days of sea sickness and I was all right again. There were about one thousand passengers from all parts of our country. I tried to fathom the motives and standing of different ones. Colonel B. from Kentucky, an aristocratic-looking man, with his slave for a body servant, who could not have been bought for less than $1,500 in Kentucky, where slavery existed at that time.[2] Why a man in his circumstances should be going to California to seek gold I could not fathom. One day a party of us were seated around the table talking matters over. It was proposed that each should reveal to the others what he expected to do and his motives for the expedition. We each related our expectations and the motives that had inspired us. My aristocratic friend was one of the party. My curiosity was at its height to know his views. He said: "Well, gentlemen, you have all been candid in your statements, and I be the same; I am going to California to deal Faro, the great American gambling game, and I don't care who knows it."

Later on in my narrative, I shall have occasion to refer to Colonel B. again under other circumstances. The fourth day out being the fourth of July, was duly celebrated on the steamer in true American style. Our course was to the east of Cuba. We passed in sight of the green hills of San Domingo to our left, and in sight of Jamaica to our right, crossing the Caribbean sea, whose grand, gorgeous sunsets I shall never forget. I could not buy a ticket in New York for the steamer from Panama to San Francisco, but was informed at the office in New York that sixty tickets were for sale in Panama by Zachrisson, Nelson & Co., the American Consul, who were agents for the steamer on the Pacific side.[3] I naturally supposed that those who offered their money first for those tickets could buy them. The price was $300 for the first cabin, and $150 for the second, from Panama to San Francisco; but a fraction of the passengers had a ticket for the Pacific side.[4]

The objective point was to get to Panama to secure a ticket, so I made an arrangement with four others; three were to take charge of the baggage of the five, and take it leisurely, and Lieutenant M., of South Carolina, and myself were selected to run an express across the Isthmus and get there ahead of the other passengers and secure tickets for the five, and try and be the first to land at Chagres.[5] We came to anchor in the bay. The captain announced that no passengers would be permitted to go ashore until the government officials had inspected the vessel. A boat came from shore with the officials. After a short stay the officials went down the side of the steamer to their boat to return to the shore. There was a guard to keep all but the proper persons from getting into the boat. I had a small carpet bag in my hand, passed the guard, slipped a $5 gold piece in his hands, and took my seat in the boat, and, of course, passed as one of the officials, and was the first passenger to land from the steamer. The first point to be made was to secure a boat for passage up the Chagres river. I was recommended to Colonel P., who was the head man in that business there.° He was a colonel in the Granadian army. I found him a full-blooded African, but an active business man in his way. I got his price for a boat and two of his best men, and then offered double the price if they would row night and day, and an extra present to the men if they made good time, for every thing seemed to depend on securing those tickets on the Pacific side. By the time I had all my arrangements made, Lieutenant M. made his appearance. He said he was the second passenger that landed from the steamer. Then behold us in what they called a dug-out, a boat somewhat similar to a canoe, with a little canopy over the center that you could crawl under to lay down with the two naked natives, with the exception of a cloth around their loins, neither understanding each other's language, to whom we could only communicate by signs. At 4 P. M., starting for Gorgona, fifty-five miles up the river, where we were to land and take mules for Panama. Eight miles was the first stopping place. We felt elated that we had got so good a start of all the other passengers. The denseness of the vegetation first attracted our attention on the banks of the river. The trees, the vines, the shrubbery, the vines clinging to the trees, hanging in all fantastic shapes, it seemed to be impenetrable, an ocean of green, unlike any thing we had ever seen before.

Early in the evening we arrived at the first stopping place, eight miles on our way up the river, where we both made ourselves at home, excited at the strangeness of the scene, surrounded by the thatched huts of the natives, who were having a dance on the square in the village. After we had been there an hour, we thought our men had their rest, and it was time to go on according to our contract, to be rowed night and day.

In the meantime it seems the natives had taken some offense

at Lieutenant M.'s familiarity, and they appeared with handles of long knives projecting back of their necks in a threatening manner. We likewise learned that that was the home of one of our men, and that he proposed to stay there all night in violation of the contract. So we had a consultation to decide what to do to get away. It was pitch dark; we laid our plan. Lieutenant M. beckoned one of the men away from the dance as if he wanted to give him something, and drew his pistol on him and marched him down to the boat, while I, with a pistol, kept him there while he went for the other man.

After a while he came with him and we got them both in the boat and started. About this time there was a storm came up with the rain, and thunder and lightning, as the elements can only perform in that way in the tropics, surrounded by impenetrable darkness, and to us an unknown river, with its serpents and alligators, with our two naked savages, that we only got in the boat by force, and, of course, could not feel very friendly toward us. Expecting to be fired on from the shore, if they could see us through the darkness, we took our departure from our first landing place on the Chagres river, surrounded by romance enough to satisfy the most romantic imagination in that line. Our men kept steadily to work. After a while the clouds broke away, the moon showed itself, and we made good progress that night. We had no trouble with our men after that. The colonel at Chagres had evidently given us his best man. They found that we were masters of the situation, and it was for their interest to submit. We treated them kindly after that, and all went well, for we passed every boat we came to. I shall never forget the look of despair of two Frenchmen, evidently gentlemen, as we went by them, and they informed us the length of time they had been coming up the river, and that they could do nothing with their men. That afternoon we came in sight of a thatched hut on the banks, evidently a ranch. We thought it for our interest to rest. We saw a man whom we took for the proprietor, entirely naked, rubbing his back against a post. On landing and approaching him he excused himself for a short time, and returned dressed, walking with the air of a lord of a manor, which dress consisted of a coarse bagging shirt, coming down to his knees. We arrived the next day at 11 A. M., at Gorgona, and took our dinner at the hotel kept by the Alcalde of the place, and bargained with him for a guide and three mules to continue our journey to Panama. As soon as our guides and mules were ready, about 1 P. M., we started for Panama. We soon got enough of our mules by being thrown a number of times over their heads. They did not understand our language. "Get up and go along," was Greek to them, but when the guide said "mula vamous" they knew what it meant. On reaching the place where we were to stay all night, we arose in the morning refreshed, but concluded to leave our mules and make the rest of the way a-foot, as we considered them a nuisance, and as we had no baggage but my little satchel previously referred to, in which I had bills of lading of my houses, they being consigned to me, the specifications of my carpenter's schedule, my letters and a gold chronometer watch, worth $250, belonging to H., a broker in New York, a friend, and a bottle of the best brandy, which he presented to me to keep off the fever in crossing the Isthmus. This bag I handed to the guide boy, about seventeen years of age, taking out the brandy bottle. The watch I was to sell, for he had two nephews who had gone to California, and if they were in need, to supply their wants. I did not meet them; sold the watch for $500 to Mr. Haight, one of the owners of the Miners' Bank in San Francisco, and remitted the money to my friend, so I shall not refer to the watch again.ᵀ

We were walking on at a free pace, our guide boy following behind. Looking back after awhile we could not see him. We stopped and waited some time, but he did not come, so we thought we would go on and he would follow. The result was we lost our way and craved for a sight of the Pacific ocean with all the ardor that Balboa could have done, the first Spanish discoverer of it, and on the same route, after our wanderings all day, almost without hope, until four in the afternoon, we came to a stream of water; oppressed with the heat of the tropics and fatigued I threw myself in the water. Lieutenant M. exclaimed: "Do not give up in that way." "I am not giving up," I replied; "only refreshing myself." In a short time he did the same thing. As we lay there we thought we heard voices. In looking back who should we see but one of our countrymen, the most gladdening sight to us. We felt saved at once. We asked him if he had any provision. He said he thought not. Then he said one of his companions might have a little piece of ham left and some crackers. He said there were three of them, and they would soon be there, and when they came one of them had some bacon and a few crackers, which he gave to us. The eating of it soon refreshed us. As I had some of the brandy left in the bottle, I extended it to them, which they were very glad to receive. Explanations ensued. We, by chance, had struck the Cruces road, and were but ten miles from Panama. They had come from Philadelphia in a brig, and had started across from Cruces, the head of boating on the Chagres river, and had been from two to three weeks getting so far across the Isthmus, and were perfectly astonished at the rapidity with which we had come. So we joined them and arrived in Panama that evening. Lieutenant M. and myself were the first of the one thousand passengers of the steamer to enter the city. The office of the agents of the Pacific steamers was closed. I went, the first thing in the morning, to purchase the five tickets for our party. Alas for human expectation! I was informed it would be several weeks before the steamer would sail. She had not yet returned from the first trip to San Francisco. They said there were but sixty tickets for sale, and they would not be offered until a few days before the departure of the steamer. Of course, all we could do was to abide our chances of getting them.' The city was walled around and dyked like those of the Middle Ages. Toward the bay the wall was one hundred feet high by twenty broad. The city had been on the decline for most a hundred years. We could see the ruins of what it once had been. At one time Spain owned all South America,

27

Mexico, California, Louisiana and Florida. Panama was the only port of entry on the Pacific coast, and controlled its commerce. As you enter the gates of the walled city there is a chapel just inside, where the lights are always burning on its altars. The first thing on entering all good Catholics enter, kneel and make their devotions, seeking the protection of the patron saint of the city. The head alcalde of the city was a Castilian Spaniard, a venerable-looking gentleman, white as any Northern man, evidently of Scandinavian descent, who ages back conquered Spain and divided the land up among themselves and became its nobility, from whom the present rulers of Spain are descendants. It is said that when conquered, the original inhabitants of Spain, to a great extent, fled to their vessels, put to sea, and found the island of Ireland, from which the present inhabitants are descendants. The second alcalder was a negro as black as I have ever seen.

In the city of Panama in its days of prosperity, when under Spain, the higher classes must have lived in great luxuries, the negroes their slaves. The natives the peons were in a condition similar to slavery, they could not leave the land as long as they owed any thing. But the despotism of old Spain became so great that when they struck for freeom, all classes united. They gave freedom to the negroes and the peons, and even the priests of the Catholic church had been so tyrannized over by the mother church in Spain that they joined the revolutionists and all classes are represented in the government. I called at a watchmaker's to have a crystal put in my watch. Two brothers had furnished rooms like a parlor. I could not speak Spanish, nor they English. I could speak a little French. I found they could speak it fluently. I asked them where they learned it. They said, "At the Jesuit college at Granada." Then one of them, when he learned that I was from the United States, went to the piano and played Hail Columbia as a compliment to my country, which would trouble most of us to do the same for their country.

There are now great trees growing up in the ruins of what was once its great cathedral. The freebooter Morgan is said to have plundered one of its altars of a million of gold and silver, and massacred many of its inhabitants, perpetrating on them the atrocities that their ancestors had upon the original natives. It is said that when Pizarro captured Peru and took the Inca, their king, prisoner, he issued a decree that if his subjects would fill a room with gold, he would release him, which they did. Instead of doing it, he sentenced him to be burned at the stake, and only commuted it to hanging on condition that he confessed the Christian religion. Madam Roland, when she was about to be guillotined in the French revolution, exclaimed, "O Liberty, what crimes have been committed in thy name." O Christianity, what terrible atrocities have been perpetrated in thy name!

Panama is a healthy city to those acclimated, facing a beautiful bay, unlike Chagres, on this side of the Isthmus of Darien, which is the most unhealthy spot on this continent. Excuse this diversion, I must get back to my subject, the days of the forty-niners.

I stopped at the American Hotel. I was somewhat in a dilapidated condition from the experiences of my trip from Chagres. The waiter in my room at the hotel took the best of care of me. I soon found he was no ordinary waiter. He had resigned a position in Washington of $2,000 a year to go to the gold Eldorado. He had been in Panama several months, and had been taken down with the fever twice, which had exhausted his funds and was working at the hotel for his board, but never thought of turning back. He was bound for California. He was quite enfeebled from the effects of the fever. He got hold of my sympathies and secured my friendship. (More of him anon.) I had been here four or five days without seeing our guide, the boy with my satchel, containing my valuables, particularly the bills of lading of my houses. I was in a quandary and anxiety about it, not knowing what to do, when one day as I was going to dinner, something pulled my coat from behind, and looking around, what should I see to my great joy and satisfaction but the native boy with my satchel, contents there all safe. It was an instance of honesty that would do honor to any nation. I gave some honest Catholic priest credit for it. The boy had evidently been instructed what to do.

The great objective point now was, how to get to San Francisco. There was no hope for a sailing vessel from this place, for we saw one return for water that had been chartered by a party that had been out three weeks, and scarcely got out of sight of the city. There is very little chance for a sailing vessel from there until they get west several hundred miles, and strike the trade winds. The chances were better with the sailing vessel to start from New York and go around Cape Horn. So the only hope seemed to be the steamer with its sixty tickets and with from one thousand to fifteen hundred passengers waiting to buy them, all seeking to bring some influence to bear to secure one. I saw in the office of the steamer agent a young man, the book-keeper, whom I took a fancy to, and sought his acquaintance. I found he was from Hudson, N. Y., and I, from Albany, both from the banks of the Hudson river. It ripened into a warm friendship. I explained my situation to him, and my desire, if it was possible, to get off on the steamer, but did not venture to ask his influence to try and get me a ticket. At this time the cholera and Panama fever was raging in full force. The unacclimated Americans were dying in every direction.[9] I was conversing at 8 A. M. with a healthy looking man, one of our passengers, from New York. At 5 P. M., the same day, I inquired for him and was informed that he was dead and buried. He had been attacked with the cholera. It was a law of the city that they must be buried within one hour after death from a contagious disease. I was finally myself taken down with the Panama fever, lay unconscious and unnoticed in my room at the hotel for a long time, and then came to and found myself burning with the raging fever, had a doctor sent for, and after a time recovered so I could venture out. In the meantime, the steamer *Panama*[10] had arrived, and its day of sailing for San Francisco announced. Zachrisson, Nelson & Co. had issued an order that the sixty tickets would be put up to be drawn for. Those having the winning numbers could have the privilege of purchasing them; that they must register their names on such a day. Probably one thousand names and but sixty tickets. The chances were small, but the only hope. On that day, I went early to register, as I was still very weak from the effects of the fever, and at my best in the morning. As I entered, there was a great number there registering. When my turn came, and I was about to put down my name, I looked behind the desk and saw my friend, the book-keeper. He shook his head for me not to. I knew that meant something favorable. I backed out. I returned at once to the hotel. In the evening, about 8 o'clock, my friend came to my room with a second cabin ticket. The joys of Paradise centered into my possession of that ticket. I asked him how did he obtain it? He said he was about to resign his position, and was going up on the same steamer to California. The night before the drawing he asked Mr. Nelson if his services had been satisfactory to him. He said they had. He then said if he should ask him a favor on leaving if he would grant it? He replied certainly. He then said that he wanted one of those sixty tickets for a particular friend. Mr. Nelson said, "If I had known what you was going to ask for, I could not have granted it; but since I have pledged my word, I shall give you the ticket."

The next day passengers would be received on the steamer, which was anchored out in the bay, some distance from shore. It was announced that no sick persons could go on the steamer. As I was quite enfeebled from my sickness, and was at my best in the morning, I thought I would make an early start, so as to be sure and be aboard, as they were all to be on board the vessel to sail early the next morning. I started out for a boat to take me out to it with the highest elasticity of feelings, not so much from the prospect of financial success as the idea that if I could get North again my physical health would be restored, and the steamer was going North. It seemed at times that I would have given $1,000 for one good breath of Northern air. As I was going along, some distance ahead of me, sitting at the doors of a doggery, with his head almost between his knees, the picture of despair, was my Washington friend, who waited on my room at the hotel when I first arrived, and did me many favors, and got hold of my sympathies. I said to myself, poor fellow, I can do nothing for you. I must not let him see me, so I dodged and passed him. When I got some distance by him my conscience smote me. I will go back and speak to him; so I did. I had advised him a few days previous to go and see some officers of the boat and offer to go up as waiter without pay. I asked him if he had done so, and what luck? He said there was no hope. They told him they had been offered $300 for the privilege of going up as waiter. I then told him I had a ticket. I was going then for a boat to go on board. That his case was desperate, and that desperate cases required desperate remedies; that he had been down twice with the fever, and the next time he would probably die; that he had no friends there nor money; if he would do as I told him I would stand by him and he must have nerve. He said to me: "How can a man have nerve without a dollar in his pocket?" which exclamation has occurred to me many times since. I asked him to hire a boat to get him out to the vessel, and what it would cost. He said $2. I gave him the money and told him to get his baggage. He said he had none. I told him to come about 11 o'clock and go to work among the hands as if he was one of them; that all were new hands and officers, and they would not know the difference. He said that the captain had said if any person was caught on board without a ticket they would be put on shore at the first uninhabited island. I told him I would attend to that in his case. I went on board and got my berth and baggage all in. About 11 o'clock I saw my friend coming over the water making for the vessel. There was considerable confusion on board at the time, passengers constantly arriving, and he was not noticed, and he went to work among the hands as if he had been regularly employed. In a short time the officers were arranging the men in line to pass the baggage, and said to him: "You stand here and help pass it," of course, taking him for one of the men of the boat.

A 'Forty-Niner.

San Francisco Temperance Society.

In the evening he came and spoke to me. I said all right so far. But in the morning, he said, they are going to examine every person, then they will put me ashore. I said, keep a stiff upper lip. If you get in trouble, come to me.

The next morning the gun fired, the anchor was raised, and we sailed down to La Boca, an island similar to Staten Island in the New York Harbor. The health officers came out. Then my friend trembled and thought the day of judgment had come to him, but the health officers were on board but a short time. No examination of those on board took place. The signal gun for departure was fired. We passed out of the harbor. The bow of our vessel was pointed north, and we felt extremely happy. I said to him, "This vessel is bound for San Francisco, and you are aboard, and will get there as soon as I will." A few days after that the mate was arranging the employment of the men, and when he came to my friend's turn he said to him, "Who employed you? You are not an able-bodied seaman." He made no reply. They could see he was a man of intelligence, and his pale look showed he had been sick. It may have moved the sympathies of the officer, who said to him, "This vessel is crowded with people; it won't do for us to be short of water, and I will put the water in your charge, and you must not let any passenger, or even the steward, have any except according to the regulations, and if you attend to that properly no other services will be required of you." That took him off of the anxious seat and put him on the solid. In all his adversities he never thought of turning back. That commanded my esteem. His attentions to me, when sick, aroused my sympathies for him, which good action on his part saved him. Of one thousand passengers desirous of getting on that steamer, and there was room but for sixty on the day of its departure; his chance looked the most hopeless, being penniless, but he was one of the fortunate ones, while those who had plenty of money were left. It illustrated the old maxim, "Where there is a will there is a way."

Nothing of interest occurred until we got to the port of Acapulco, the largest place on the west coast of Mexico. We were about to enter the harbor when a government boat with officials came out and ordered us to stop. If we proceeded any further there would be "matter of trouble" in broken English. There were Americans on shore who had crossed over from Vera Cruz for the purpose of taking this streamer. It would be a month before there would be another one, and then there would be no certainty of their getting aboard of that. The captain held a consultation of the passengers, who all decided to have them come on board. They were our countrymen and we would share our berths with them, although the vessel was then crowded, and some of the passengers volunteered to row ashore with the small boats to bring them aboard, which they did. When they approached the shore there was a company of soldiers waded in the water with pointed guns, forbidding them to approach any nearer. The Americans who were on the bank informed them that the soldiers would fire, and warning them not to approach any nearer, while bewailing their fate that they had to be left, so they returned. Then the captain received notice to leave in half an hour or the guns of the fort would open fire on us. It was a bright moonlight night. The fort was on a high knoll just above us, and could have blown us out of the water. So we thought discretion was the better part of valor, and we had to leave. The laws of nations were on their side. We were from an infected port, Panama, where cholera prevailed."

O N BOARD THE steamer were some men of prominence. W. F. Macondray, from Boston, a retired East India sea captain, a man of wealth, who had been out of business for three years and craved for a more exciting life; who started the largest commission-house in San Francisco, and had consigned to him about all the shipments from Boston, and likewise, the *Prince de Joinville* with my houses; Mr. G., from Liverpool, an Englishman, who had about all the consignments from that city;

Rothschild's nephew, who had represented that house as a banker in Valparaiso, Chili, was going to establish a branch of those great bankers' house in San Francisco; Judge Terry, from Louisiana, who had the reputation at that time of being a dead shot with a pistol, who afterward challenged United States Senator Broderick to fight a duel, from political influences, and killed him, and some years afterward was assassinated himself from a disagreement with parties about a lawsuit.[12] We came opposite Mazatlan at the mouth of the Gulf of California, and took on board some passengers and freight.

The next incident in our voyage was when we came in sight of San Diego, California, and saw the American flag floating from the flag staff. There was an instantaneous shout went up from every American on board. We were once more to be under its protection in our own country.

> Love of country, mystic fire from heaven,
> To light our race up to stateliest heights 'tis given.

We were entering the Golden Gate. It was but four miles to the harbor where we cast anchor, opposite the city of San Francisco, which was the goal of our hopes for so long a time, and which was about to be realized; which was also the objective point from almost every part of the world where adventurers are seeking to get. We had come three thousand, five hundred miles since we left Panama. We engaged a row-boat to take us ashore. My friend attended to getting my baggage out of the boat, and went with me to the shore. He had signed no papers, and entered into no bonds not to desert the vessel at San Francisco, as the other sailors had. He was free to do as he pleased.

I had the chills and fever all the way up, from the effects of the Panama fever. My first idea was to get in good quarters, whatever expense, to regain my health. I was informed that there was a good hotel kept by a widow woman on Montgomery street, where we landed. Some of the other passengers were going to stop there. I inquired the terms. They said $5 per day. I thought

I would try it for a while. My sleeping-room was a mattress laid on the floor, with muslin partitions to separate us from the next room. The table was very indifferent, no vegetables, which I required, which we lacked on the ship coming up. Being in poor health, I needed them. After being there a few days one of our passengers asked me if I knew what the charges were. I said yes, $5 per day. He said it was more; I had better ask again, which I did. I was informed it was $5 for the room and extra for the meals. I paid my bill and looked out for other quarters. I had brought in my baggage an Indian rubber mattress and pillow which was folded up in a small space and could be blown up with your breath and filled with air, made a soft bed, a pair of new Mackinaw blankets and other things to provide for any contingency, and took meals at a restaurant, which were numerous, including the Chinese which we often patronized, and found myself satisfactorily quartered. It may not be inappropriate to make some general remarks about the history of California.

Although my subject is strictly on the days of forty-niners, which consisted of about two years from the discovery of the gold, when it was supposed that the future prosperity of the country depended exclusively on the mining interest. How different it has turned out since has nothing to do with my subject. I want to try to paint to the mind of the reader the condition of California at that time, and the views of the pioneers in those days. I was doing it in the form of a personal narrative, as it enables me more distinctly to recall to my mind the events of those days in which I was a participant. Such fluctuations of fortune as then occurred, the world never saw before in the same space of time, and probably never will again, where common labor was $16 per day. There were some very interesting and truthful articles published in the *Century* magazine two years ago from the pen of the pioneers, but there has been no book published as a standard work for the present and future, and the participants in it are passing away, for it is forty-five years since they occurred. California is three times larger in territory than the State of New York. Its population before the discovery of gold, including Indians and all, was but a few thousand. Cattle could be bought for $1 per head, and all the land they ranged upon thrown in the bargain for nothing. They were killed for their hides, and the meat thrown away, as there was no one to eat it.

A Few Historical Items.

San Francisco bay, first discovered the 25th of October, 1769. The first ship that ever entered the harbor was the *San Carlos,* June, 1775. The mission of Dolores founded by the Jesuit Fathers in 1769.[13] Colonel Jonathan Stevenson arrived at California with one thousand men on the 7th of March, 1847. The treaty of Hidalgo ceding California to the United States by Mexico, officially proclaimed by the president, July 4, 1848. Gold first discovered by Marshall, January 9, 1848.[14] January, 1848, the whole white population of California was fourteen thousand, January, 1849, the population of San Francisco was two thousand. The three most prominent publicmen at the time of my arrival in California were Colonel Frémont, who had conducted an expedition overland; Colonel Stevenson, who came by sea with one thousand men, appointed by William L. Marcy, who was secretary of war during the conflict with Mexico, from whom I had a letter of introduction as a family connection of Governor Marcy, similar to the following letter to Brigadier Major-General P. F. Smith, which was not delivered:

Albany, *June 24, 1849.*

My Dear Sir—I desire to present to your favorable notice, the bearer hereof, Dr. Daniel Knower. He is on the eve of departing for California. He is a family connection of mine, a gentleman of talents and respectability, and I commend him to your favorable notice.

Yours truly,

William L. Marcy.

Brig.-Gen. P. F. Smith.

I soon found the colonel one of the warmest of friends. Captain John A. Sutter, who was a captain in the Swiss Guards of Charles the Tenth of France, after the revolution of 1830 in that country, came to the United States, who some years previous had wandered across the country to Oregon, and the Russian Fur Company secured for him a large grant of land from Mexico in California, on which the city of Sacramento now stands, extending back from that city many miles to where the gold was first discovered. He was having a raceway dug on the American river for the purpose of erecting a saw-mill, as there was no lumber in the country. He had constructed a fort some miles back from the Sacramento river, where he made his home.[15] The object of the Russian Fur Company was to have a place where they could purchase grain, as there was none raised there at that time, and they had a contract with him, and that they were to send a vessel at such a time, and he was to settle up the country and cultivate it. Sutter was the most social and generous of men. The latch-string of his cabin was always on the outside, and all callers were welcome, and the hospitalities of the fort extended to all callers.

At the time of my arrival in California in '49, there were several hundreds of ships anchored in the bay deserted by their crews, who had gone to the mines. They could make more in one day there than their wages would amount to in a month on the vessel.

In the city a large portion of its population were living in tents. There were not buildings enough. Vessels were constantly arriving loaded with people from all parts of the world. As my health permitted I investigated matters there. I took a walk out. I met what looked like a laboring man. I asked him how long he had been there? He said two months. I said to him: "And not gone up to the mines yet?" He said to me he was in no particular hurry. He said he had a row-boat and made $20 a day rowing passengers to and from the vessels (there was then no dock). He had his boy with him, who gathered mussels and sold them.

38

Between the two they averaged $30 per day, which explained why he was in no hurry to go to the gold diggings.

Lumber was bringing fabulous prices. It looked very favorable for my house ventures. Mr. G., the Englishman, had been very anxious to buy them. He had seen the specifications of the carpenter on the steamer coming up. On Saturday P.M. I called at his office. He asked me if I had made up my mind to sell him the houses. I said to him: "If I should put a price on them you would not take me up." He said "try me." I named a price. He said he would take them and go to my lawyer to draw up the contract. I said I would just as soon go to his (which was a fatal mistake). I knew his was a State senator from Florida, and had come up on the steamer with us. We found the lawyer in his office, and he commenced drawing up the contract. I made my statement that I sold the houses from my carpenter's specifications (not from any representations I made myself), and from the bills of lading and from my insurance policy, which ranked the ship *Prince de Joinville,* formerly a Havre packet, classed A, No. 1. He was to deposit bills of lading of the ship *St. George* from Liverpool, consigned to him, in value to the amount of $50,000, with a third party, as collateral security, that on the arrival of the *Prince de Joinville,* and the delivery of the houses, he was to pay me the sum agreed upon.

The lawyer, after writing a little, complained of a headache, and asked if it made any difference if he put it off until Monday morning. I said, Mr. G. had been very anxious to buy the houses, and I had not cared about selling them to arrive, preferring to take my chances when the vessel got here, but since I had consented to sell them, I preferred to have it on the solid. I said, I supposed the transaction was not of great importance to Mr. G., but I had all that I was worth in the world at stake on the venture, and would prefer to have it closed now. He commenced writing, and again complained of the headache. I then consented to put it off until Monday morning at 10 o'clock. We both pledged our

39

honor to meet there at that time and consummate it. I was there on Monday morning at the time designated. Mr. G. came in at 11 o'clock and said he had changed his mind and would not take the houses. I said all right, but his word of pledge of honor would have no value with me thereafter.

I would have made $18,000 profit, but I was selling them for a good deal less than they would have brought if they had been there. Lumber was selling as high as from three to four hundred dollars per thousand feet in San Francisco at that time. But I was making certain of a good profit and running no risk of what might happen in the future.

I had another offer of a number of lots on Stockton street, the next street above the plaza in the heart of the city, for six of the smaller ones, which, if I had consummated, would have made my fortune. "There is a tide in the affairs of men, which, if taken at the flood tide, leads on to fortune, or, if not seized, are forever lost." (Shakespeare.)

The ideas of the people there at that time was, that a railroad across the continent, connecting California with the East, was entirely impracticable. That there were one thousand miles of desert to cross, where there was no water, and the Sierra Nevada mountains presented an impassable barrier, and they thought how could it ever be an agricultural country, when there was no rain for more than seven months in the year. The idea of irrigation was not thought of then. How different every thing has turned out since, I have nothing to do with. I must be true to my subject, the days of the Forty-niners.

As it would be, at least, three months before the ship could come in with my houses, and my health had improved, I was anxious to get up to the mines. I was informed that there was a party from Albany at the Dutch bar, on the south fork of the American river, about eight miles from Coloma, where gold was discovered, with whom I was acquainted. I found a sloop about to sail for Sacramento (there were no steamers then) the starting point to the northern mine. I took passage on board with all the passengers the boat could accommodate. I noticed on the passage up that the mosquitoes were very large, with penetrating bills. It was as much as we could do to protect our faces.

The only important event on the passage was that a man had potatoes that he was taking up on speculation, and that he was going to treat his fellow passengers to some, one day at dinner. We were a little disappointed when we found they were sweet ones, but still they were a treat. Vegetables were scarce, potatoes selling from forty to sixty cents per pound. After a few days we arrived at Sacramento, it being about one hundred miles from San Francisco by water. There were no hacks at the landing, nobody that wanted a job to carry your baggage. Governor Shannon, of Ohio, was among the passengers.[16] He had been minister to Mexico, yet he had to carry his own baggage, and make several trips to do it. One of the passengers assisted him. He was president of a mining company organized in Ohio.

I T WAS EVENING, so we stopped at a hotel, and I slept in my Mackinaw blanket that I carried with me, on the dining-room floor. The next morning after breakfast, about 9 o'clock, I went out on the front portico to take observations of the place. The landlord was there. There was a loaferish-looking fellow going by on the opposite side of the street. The landlord cries out to him: "Bill, what will you charge to chop wood for me from now until night?" He cries back, "What will you give?" He replies, "$10." Bill answers back, "Can't chop for less than an ounce," which was $16, and walked right on. It was evident that common labor was not suffering there for want of employment.

I was there some days, and could find no one to post me how to get to Coloma. All was excitement and bustle. While there, Sam. Brannan—who had built a new hotel there (just finished), called the City Hotel—gave a free entertainment for one day to the public. He must have expended $1,000 for refreshments. He had been a Mormon preacher, and was a captain in Colonel

Stevenson's regiment. He was very enterprising and generous, a prominent figure with the "Forty-niners.""

I saw an article in the paper a few years ago from a California correspondent, giving a biography of him; that he was, at one time, worth several millions, and went into some big enterprise —which I cannot now recall—and was unfortunate and lost all his wealth, and that he was, at that time, in San Francisco at a twenty-five-cent lodging-house, and that he told him that he passed two men that day who had crossed the street to avoid him, to whom he had furnished the money from which they had made their fortunes.

Well, I finally found an Oregon man with a yoke of oxen, who was freighting goods up to Coloma. He said he had seven hundred and fifty acres of land in Oregon, but no cattle on it. He thought he would come to California and get gold enough to buy them, and his wife was keeping a cake and pie stand on the streets of that city. I never saw him after that trip, but coming with so modest expectations, I have no doubt he was successful.

We started on our journey in the afternoon. The country through which we traveled looked as if it had been an old-settled land, and deserted by its inhabitants. It seemed that we must come to a farm-house, but there was none. There were scattering trees in the country and occasionally a woods, but no dense forest. We made eight miles, then camped for the night on the edge of a woods. I had brought no provisions with me, so I offered him $1 per meal to eat with him, which was accepted. He made tea, cooked some Indian meal, and had a jug of molasses; so we made a very good supper. I got my satchel out of the wagon for a pillow, and with my blankets made my bed on the ground under the wagon. I though it would keep the dew off, but there was none.

There is no danger of taking cold sleeping on the ground in the dry season, when it does not rain for seven months. He had set fire to a dead tree to keep the grizzly bears off, and about the time I got comfortably laid down, there was a pack of coyote wolves came howling around. Amid those surroundings, the burning of the fire to keep the grizzlies off and howling of the wolves, I fell asleep and did not wake until morning, refreshed from my slumbers. After a breakfast similar to the meal the night before, we proceeded on our journey, but the ox team travelled so slow that in walking I got away ahead of it, and then got tired of waiting for it to come up to me, and so went on alone. Toward night I came to Mormon Island, the first gold diggings. I inquired if there was a place where I could get quarters for the night. They said I might, at the hospital. It was a log cabin with bunks in it, and what was my astonishment to find the proprietor, a doctor from Troy, N. Y., an old acquaintance.[18] I was more than welcome. We were both delighted to see each other. I to find such comfortable quarters, and he to meet with a friend in the wilderness, and to hear the latest news from the East. He got for me the best supper that the surroundings would afford; as I had eaten nothing since morning; it was very acceptable, and he provided for me the most comfortable of his bunks for sleeping. He informed me that it was twenty-five miles from Coloma, and there was but one place on the way where I could get water to drink. I started after breakfast, refreshed. After travelling some miles, I came to the smoke of the camp-fire of Indians, just ahead of me. It was rumored that the Oregon men were in the habit of shooting an Indian on sight when they had a chance.[19] The Indians killed white men in retaliation, as they could not make peace until they had killed as many whites as they had lost, according to their ideas of equity. As I did not care particularly about being one to make up the number, I struck off in a ravine and passed around so as to avoid their camping ground and came to the road beyond them. What truth there was about the shooting of them I could not say, but it was currently reported at the time. About 4 o'clock, P. M., I got to a stopping place six miles from Coloma. There I met a man with a long beard, slouched hat, a sash around his body, a flannel shirt, evidently a miner. I had a long talk with him. He posted me about the gold diggings and I him about the news from the States. As we were about to part, he asked me to take a drink. He inquired of the proprietor if he had champagne? He said, yes, at $10 a bottle. The man said, pass us down a bottle, which we drank together. He, evidently, had struck good diggings. We parted, as I was anxious to get to Coloma before dark, having made twenty-five miles in one day on foot. I found a regular tavern here, kept by a man from Mississippi, with his family. I sat down to a regular table for my supper, which seemed quite a treat. He informed me that he had no bed-room for me; that I could sleep on the dining-room floor, or in his barn. He had just had some new hay put in. I chose the latter. It was a kind of a shanty building, but the soft bed of new hay was a luxury after my twenty-five mile walk.

I awoke the next morning refreshed. After my breakfast I took in the place and went to the raceway where the first piece of gold was discovered. There were three or four stores in the place to supply miners of the surrounding region. I got my direction how to find the Dutch Bar, eight miles from there. Proceeding on my way, after going about five miles, I came to a person, his face covered with a long beard, whom I recognized, by the expression of his eyes, as a person who I knew in Albany, and who belonged to the party I was seeking. He informed me that I was within three miles of them, and he gave me plain directions how to find them. I soon came to their camp and there was a genial meeting and exchange of news. There were five in the company. They had a tent and owned a pair of mules. I joined them, as I had not come to depend on mining, as I never had been accustomed to physical labor. At first I thought it was awful hard work, and that it was lucky for me that I had not come to California depending on it, but after a short time I got used to it and liked it. They took turns in cooking, so each one had one day in the week that he did the cooking. We lived on fried pork and flapjacks made from wheat flour fried in the fat of the pork, tin cups for our tea and coffee, and tin dishes.

We each had stone seats, and a big one in the center for our table. At night we slept under our tent. The gold rivers were not navigable. They were sunk way down deep in the earth. When the rainy season sets in during the winter months, and sometimes rains every day in the month, causing the snow to melt on the Sierra Nevada mountains, where these streams take their rise, will cause the water to rise often from ten to twenty feet in a night, and in the course of ages has worn their depth down into the earth, and is supposed to have washed out of the earth the scales of gold that are found on the banks of the rivers. The first mining was a very simple process. A party of three could work together to the best advantage. A virgin bar was where the river had once run over and now receded from it. Three persons worked together, one to clear off the sand on the ground to within six inches of the hard-pan. The top earth was not considered worth washing, the scales of gold, being heavier, had settled through it, but could not penetrate that portion of the earth called the hardpan, so the earth within six inches of it was impregnated with more or less gold, and one to carry the bucket to the rocker, and the other to run the rocker, which was located close to the water. The rocker was a trough about three feet in length with three slats in it and a sieve at the upper end, on which the bucket of earth was thrown. The man worked the rocker with one hand and dipped the water out of the river with a tin-handled dipper. As he worked the rocker the fine earth and scales of gold passed through the holes of the sieve and settled behind the slats in the trough, and the stones and large lumps in which there was no gold were caught in the sieve and thrown away. After a certain number of buckets of earth had been run through in that way, the settlings behind the slats in the trough were put in a milk-pan and the water was allowed to run in the pan and the fine earth and sand would float on the top of the water. You would let that run off.

After a few operations of that kind you would see the yellow scales of gold on the edge of the sand. You would continue that

45

process until there was but a little of the sand left; then you would take it with you when you went to the tank and warm it by a fire to dry the sand; then with your breath you would blow away the sand and have the gold, which you carried in a buckskin bag, which was the currency of the country, at $16 per ounce, and at the mint in Philadelphia was worth $18.25. I have carried three hundred buckets in a day, and at twenty-five cents worth of gold in a bucket, it would amount to $75, $25 to each man for his day's work, which was frequently the average.[20] In those days all it cost for a party of three for capital to start mining was about $15. Then you had the chances of striking a pocket. That was a cavity in the rocks where gold had settled. In the course of ages, and where the strong currents of the streams, when the rivers were high, could not reach it to wash it out, I have known a person to take out $800 of gold in less than an hour. The first miners, when they found gold on the banks of the river, thought if they could only dig in the deep holes of the bed they would find chunks of it, and they went to a big expense, and those who had money hired laborers to assist in constructing raceways at $16 per day, to change the current of the river; but when they had effected their object and dug there they found no gold, for there was nothing to prevent the strong current from carrying it off; but I knew a party to draw off the water and expose the bed of the river, where there were rapids, and they were successful, and the gold had settled down between the crevices of the rocks, and the currents could not disturb it.

There were some other kinds of diggings discovered different from the river mining, called cañons, one I know of, called the Oregon. It was described like a tunnel, deep down in the earth, where a party of three persons from near our locality went and returned in about three weeks and had from three to five thousand dollars apiece, which they showed me. It was not scale gold, but nuggets of all sizes. Of course, they had unusual luck.

On the river mining each person was entitled to so many feet, as long as they left any implements of labor on it. No person would trespass upon it; but if he took every thing away, then it was inferred he had given it up, and anybody had a right to take it. All regulations were strictly respected and every thing was safe, and a person told me that he would not be afraid to leave his bag of gold in his tent. Every thing was honorable and safe until the overland emigrants from western Missouri arrived there. They were a different kind of people; more of the brute order. When they saw a party of two or three that had a good claim, and they were the strongest, they would dispossess them. (I suppose the same class that raided Kansas in John Brown's time.) They became so obnoxious that a respectable man would deny his State.

And another corrupt element arrived by sea, the ex-convicts from Sidney.

I went to Coloma one day to get supplies for the party. I rode one of the mules, the other followed to be packed with the purchases. When I bought what was wanted, I handed the storekeeper my bag of gold to pay him. When he returned it to me, I found his statement made was between three and four dollars less than I knew was in it. I informed him of the discrepancy. He said he did not see how that could be; that he weighed it right. He came in in a few minutes and apologized, saying that he had weighed it in the scales that he used when he traded with the Indians. It needs no comment to know that the Christian man is not always superior to the Indian in integrity. There was an Indian who had struck a pocket. He came to Coloma with $800 in gold dust that he got out in a short time. He invested it all with the storekeepers in a few hours. He had dressed himself in the height of fashion, including a gold watch. He was dressed as no California Indian ever had been before. The gold he could not eat nor drink.

How the gold came there is one of the mysteries of nature. One theory is, that the Sierra Nevada mountains were once the banks of the Pacific ocean, and all California had been thrown up from the bottom of the sea from that depth where gold was

47

a part of the formation of the earth, in connection with quartz, and as all gold appears in a molten state, which would go to corroborate this theory. A person informed me that he went through a ravine where one side of the road was half of a large rock, and on the other side, the other half. He could see where the two halves would match each other exactly.

Well, I lived that life for two months. We had an addition to what I have described to eat—pork and beans on Sunday, and Chili pudding. It had been baked and sweetened, and then ground up like flour and put in bags. All you had to do was to moisten it with water to eat it. All our flour came from that country, put up in sacks of fifty and one hundred pounds each, but we had no vegetables. One day we heard that they had dried-apple sauce at the hotel at Coloma for dinner. The next day, Sunday, three of us walked eight miles to get there to dinner to get a taste of it. We paid $2 apiece for our dinner, and they had the sauce; it tasted so good that we did not begrudge the price of the dinner and the walk back again. We were fully satisfied.

The rainy season set in. It rained three days, and although it was three or four weeks before it would be possible for my houses to arrive, yet it was a new country and no bridges. The streams might get up so as to be impassable, and the houses were consigned to me, and no one but myself to receive them. I thought I had better get back to San Francisco at once. What I was making in the mines was mere nothing to what I had at stake in the houses. Although, to tell the truth, I never left a place with more regret, as hard as the fare was. We were interested every day in the work for gold, and did not know when we might make a rich strike. My last day there it rained. Notwithstanding, a companion and myself went out to dig for a couple of hours. When we returned, we had $25 worth. That was the last of my mining. I started the next morning for Sacramento afoot. I sold my pistol and blankets for an ounce each, $16 apiece. On my route I met a man bound for the same place. We joined teams and became very intimate.

Selling Off.

In the Lap of Luxury.

The only incident of importance was when we got within five miles of Sacramento. We stopped at a log cabin and ordered dinner. A short time after my companion came to me in some excitement and said he had looked through a window and that they were cooking potatoes for dinner. I could not believe the good news, and so went and looked for myself and found it was true. I had not tasted one in two months. We took the steamer *Senator* that evening for San Francisco.²¹ It had been a Long Island steamboat and had arrived since my departure for the mines. It was the first steamer that had ever sailed the interior waters of California, and had been put on to run from San Francisco to Sacramento. I think it belonged to Grenell, Minton & Co., a prominent shipping firm of New York city. Charley Minton had charge of it. Of course its profits were great. But I could not sleep in my state-room berth; I had been so long used to a hard bed I was restless, but we arrived safe the next morning at San Francisco. The bulk of my book will be events that occurred during my residence in that city. I scarcely know how to begin to describe it. My efforts will be to portray them truthfully. To do so I must continue in the form of a personal narrative. That is the only way I can recall the events to my mind of so long ago.

At this time more changes took place there in a month than in most any other place in a year. Every thing was done by the month. Buildings were rented by the month; money was loaned by the month; ten per cent per month was the regular interest. There was but one bank, called the Miners', on the corner of the plaza, owned by three parties. During my absence a great boom had taken place—influenced by new arrivals and most favorable news from the gold mining sections. This was the fall of 1849. The lots that I had thought of trading six of my houses for had tripled in value, but lumber was still bringing fabulous prices and every thing looked favorable for a big strike on my houses when they arrived. Montgomery street was on the banks of the bay. There was one pier at this time constructed from it in the bay, and a temporary pier by Colonel Stevenson at the north beach. The city was growing toward Happy Valley.[22] Portsmouth Square, the plaza, still had some of the adobe buildings on it. The best hotel was the Parker House, on the west corner of it. The plaza was sand, no vegetation on it.

Rincon Point, on Telegraph Hill, was the spot where ships and steamers were signalled.[23] Steamers coming in but once a month, they brought the last news from the East. The New York papers were peddled at $1 each. Long lines of people were formed to get the mail, and you had to take sometimes half a day before you could reach the office. Oakland, opposite the bay, had no existence. Goat Island had no existence. Goat Island had plenty of wild goats on it, and we could never imagine how the first goat ever got there. There was no scarcity of meat— plenty of beef and grizzly bears were hung out at the doors of the restaurants as a sign, and plenty of venison. I can recall now to my mind, venison steaks that we would get in the evening with their rich jellies on it. The luxuries of Asia were coming in there. Many China restaurants with their signs from Canton or Pekin. But there was a great scarcity of vegetables. Onions and potatoes sold for forty cents per pound.

A day or two after my arrival, my friend who came down with me from the mines came to me and said that there were a lot of blankets to be sold at auction; that he had no money, or he would buy them; that if I would buy them he would take them up in the mines and peddle them out for me for half of the profit. As I knew they were in great demand there—I had sold, when I left there, mine for $16—I told him if he could buy them for $4 per pair to bid them off and I would furnish the money to pay for them. He came back in a short time and said he had bought them, and that they came to $800. We had them taken to the steamer *Senator* to ship to Sacramento. We paid $10 a load to have them carted from the store where they were bought to the steamer. (The result of this speculation later on.)

There were at this time several hundred vessels anchored in the bay, deserted by their officers and crews. A ship could be bought for probably one-third of what it was worth in New York, and I conceived the project of buying a ship as soon as I sold my houses, which I expected soon to arrive, being on so fast a ship as the *Prince de Joinville,* and going myself to the Sandwich Islands and buying a load of onions and potatoes, as I was informed that they could be bought as cheap there as in the States, and ciphered out that one successful venture of that kind would make my fortune. So I went among the idle ships to see what I could do in that line, and to have one selected, ready to close the bargain as soon as the houses arrived. I came across a brig that had been running to Sacramento, but was condemned as a foreign bottom, when Collier, the collector, arrived there, a short time before, and extended the marine laws of the United States over California.[24] The captain and crew were aboard. The capain was an Englishman; the crew, cosmopolitan—a Hindostan, a Mexican named Edwin Jesus, an English sailor and an American. I inquired of the captain about the history of the vessel. He said she had been built at Guayaquil, down the coast, and had belonged to a Mexican general, and was built partially of an American whaler that had been wrecked on the coast, so I got American timbers in her. They wanted to sell the vessel. I told him I might buy her. I would let them know in a day or two. So I went to Colonel Stevenson and gave him a history of it, and asked him if he would see Collier, the collector of the port, and see if I could not get her papers as an American vessel, which he did, and informed me the next day that it was all right. I went at once and bought the brig. As soon as I got its American papers it was worth twice what I had to pay for it. I kept the same captain, as he knew the navigation of the rivers, which few did at that time. I gave him $250 per month and put a supercargo at $150 per month, and kept the same crew. I had it put up for Stockton, the head depot for the Southern mines. The first month it made two trips. Its receipts were $3,100; its expenses, $1,100; so it earned me $2,000 clear.

There was a friend of mine named R., who owned a third interest in a factory that belonged to a relative of mine who got the gold fever when I did, and got me to negotiate the sale of his interest in it to him, which I did for $8,000, so he could go to California with me.[25] When he arrived there he proposed to build a brewery. His father had been a brewer in Scotland. He bought a lot, a part of the city called Happy Valley, and started to build the first brewery on the Pacific coast. He commenced to build one that would cost $30,000 with that capital, which was his mistake. If he had commenced in a small way he would have made his fortune. (In my personal narrative he had much to do with my affairs.)

AT THIS POINT in writing my manuscript, I have just heard of the death of Colonel Jonathan Stevenson, aged ninety-four, in California, to whom I had a letter of introduction from Governor William L. Marcy.[26] I found him the warmest, the truest and most generous friend. He was a little unpopular when I first met him, for what I conceived the most noble action of his life. There were in his regiment roughs from the city of New York, where it was organized, who, when the war was over with Mexico, would go into saloons and places and help themselves to what they wanted and refused to pay. They were termed "The Hounds." There was a vigilance committee organized against them, which public sentiment, at that time, fully indorsed. They had seized a number of them and were about to hang them. Colonel Stevenson faced the excited crowd and asked to have them give the men a trial and punish the guilty. He said that when he returned to New York and their mothers asked him what had become of their sons, how could he face them if they were put to death in that way; but if he could say to them that they had a fair trial, were found guilty of crime, and had been punished according to law, it would be different. I think they were not executed, but banished; but it set up a cry against the colonel that he had taken the part of "The Hounds," so unjust is often, for a time, public sentiment.[27] That was the first vigilance committee; the great one came afterward, but I am confined to the days of the "Forty-niners."

It was rumored, at the time, that there was a jealousy between him and Colonel Frémont. It was not on the part of Stevenson. I boarded at the same hotel with Frémont.

The colonel asked me one day to speak to Frémont at dinner, and request him, if convenient, to stop in his office as he came from dinner, which I did. Stevenson's office was on the plaza, but Frémont never called.

There was great difficulty about the title to lots at that time. There were contentions set up, and claims of property from different Mexican grants, as it became valuable. It was guaranteed by the United States, at the treaty of Hidalgo, when California was ceded to us, that all titles that were good under the Mexican government should be recognized by us. L., the chaplain of Stevenson's regiment, seems to have been the butt of the boys before the gold was discovered.[28]

They, as a farce, elected him alcalde of San Francisco, which position is a combination of mayor and judge, as we would understand it, and his election was declared illegal. Then they elected him for spite. He served one year. There was a Mexican law that in any village in that country a person had a right to settle on one hundred veras of land so many feet, about three hundred, and if he put up any kind of a building on it, and held undisputed possession for one year, he could go to the alcalde, and by paying $16, get a good and valid title.[29] When the lots became so valuable in San Francisco, after the gold was discovered, many lots based on those kinds of grants became very valuable two or three years after the discovery of gold. L. became quite wealthy, it was said, by advances in real estate. There were

53

rumors of bogus titles in the names of dead soldiers and others who had left the country, but could be traced to no authentic source. He was estimated to be worth several hundred thousand dollars, made in the rise of real estate. I met him but once and I sold him some lumber.

My shipping merchant who negotiated freight for my brig got a legal title of that kind.

He said he was a book-keeper for a firm in Newport, Rhode Island, at small salary. He made up his mind that if they would not raise his pay $100 per year on the 1st of January he would leave them. They refused, so he lost his situation, and it was dull times, and he could not get another one, so he shipped on a whaling vessel as a sailor. His health was poor, and he found he could not stand the hardships of that life. The vessel put in the harbor of San Francisco for water and fresh meat on their way to the Arctic ocean, so he deserted the ship and secreted himself until it left. Then he had to do something there for a living, so he squatted on one hundred veras of land on the beach, and put up a shanty and sold fruit and probably some liquor, etc., to make a living. No one disturbed him for one year. He applied to the alcalde and paid his $16 and got a good, valid title. After the gold was discovered it became the most valuable property in the city. When I was doing business with him he had a three-story brick store, which he owned. The whaling ship had been gone to the Arctic ocean two or three years and had heard nothing of the discovery of the gold, and wonderful changes in San Francisco, and the captain thought he would put in that port on his return and hunt up his runaway sailor, and behold, his absconding sailor was rich enough when he found him to buy his ship and his whole cargo of whale oil. I was introduced by him to his captain and shook hands with him, and we had a good talk over it. Wherein does our stories of fiction, of our boyhood, of Arabian Nights, surpass the actual events of life, of the wonderful fluctuations of fortunes in California in the days of the Forty-niners?

On the death of President Taylor, a meeting was called for the purpose of having a funeral obsequies there in his honor. A man was named for president of the day. Then it was proposed to name a vice-president for each State and Territory, which was done. There were persons in the crowd from every one of them. A day was set apart for the ceremonies, and all business was to be suspended. There was a long procession on that day, and the masons and all societies and the people in general turned out in full force, including the Chinese, who were smart enough to think it would make a favorable impression in their favor. After the parade was dismissed in the plaza, the Chinese were requested to remain, and a missionary addressed them, and a Chinaman interpreted to them in their own language. I noticed that their language was much more condensed than ours. It took about a third of the time for him to translate what the missionary said. When the missionary closed, he said he hoped that we would all meet together in another and a better world. It seemed to them so absurd that they looked at each other and smiled as if it was a good joke.[30]

In those early days there were no particular prejudices against them. Pagans, as we call them, practised the Christian virtues toward their own countrymen. When the ship arrived from China they were down to greet the newcomers, whom they had never seen before, and invite them to their homes. The present laws of restriction against them, I think, are all right. We cannot afford to run the risk of having the institutions of our country injured by an emigration that is uncongenial to it. We have gone too far in that line already, not from selfishness, but to perpetuate the institutions founded by our revolutionary ancestors, in their purity, for the interests of mankind.

I received a letter from my blanket friend. He informed me that he could not sell the blankets, and had traded them off for flour, and would start the next day for the Yuba, which was the most remote gold river. That was a lie. He did that so that I would not follow him up. He had not a dollar invested in them.

They were my property. I knew at once I had been dealing with a rascal, but I was powerless to do anything about it, so I wrote him back that it was all right; that I had bought a brig; and that I had it running to Stockton, and he could take ventures up on that and make up what we had lost on the blankets, and much more. (More of him later on.)

THE GAMBLING OF THAT DAY.

It was public most everywhere. Faro tables, the great American gambling game, Monte, the Mexican and Roulette. The Eldorado, on the corner of the plaza, was the most celebrated gambling house of that time. There had been a great deal of money expended in fitting it up. It had an orchestra of fifteen persons. It was run all night and day, with two sets of hands. It was gorgeously fitted up. What they used to stir up the sugar in the drinks cost $300. It was solid gold. Numerous gambling tables, piled up with gold and silver, to tempt the bettor, behind which were hired dealers. The owners of the Eldorado were not known. Many a miner has come with his few thousand dollars to San Francisco to sail for home, and taking in the sights, visited the Eldorado, got interested in the different games, and lost it all and went back to the gold regions broken and penniless to try his luck over again. I heard of one that lost his all three times in that way. I saw a man once put down a bag of gold, which contained $5,000, bet $1,000 on one turn of the card at Monte. He lost. While I was looking at him in the course of half an hour, he lost it all. I thought what independence that amount would have given some family in the East.

In those early days there was often but a muslin partition between you and the next room, and you could hear every word in the next apartment. About 1 o'clock in the morning I was awaken by two men entering and taking the next room to mine, whom I saw running a Roulette table on the plaza. They seemed to be considerably excited. They said they would be willing to lose some money to get rid of that tapper. Of course, I could not understand, at first, what they meant by that expression, but come to find out from their conversation, they had their Roulette table arranged so that they could make the ball stop on the red or black, as it happened to be for their interest to have it do. So, if there were $20 bet upon the red, the tapper would bet $10 on the black, and they could not make the red lose without making the black win. So the tapper was getting half of their gains. I would advise all my friends to let Roulette alone, unless they are sure they can place themselves in the position of the tapper.

One morning on the plaza I took a look into a gambling saloon. I saw a Greaser that had been betting against Monte all night, and had had wonderful luck. He announced that he would tap the bank for $1,800, which was more money than he ever had before, or could ever expect to have again, which meant that he would bet that amount for whatever sum the dealer could show to meet it on the turn of one card. He lost, and the dealer showed $1,800 in the bank and took all his money. Monte is the great National gambling game of Mexico, and his idea of Paradise is to be able to break a Monte bank.

Mr. B. from Kentucky, whom I took for so rich a nabob, referred to among the passengers when out of New York. I saw him take out his gold watch, a valuable one, and bet it behind the queen, on the game of Faro, for $100. He was evidently about broke. It won. Then he went the $200 and it won again. Then he went it the third time, and it won. In about twenty minutes he had his watch back and $700, then he left. Some one asked me a few months after that if I knew that he was worth $80,000? He had been very lucky, and that he was to run for sheriff of San Francisco county on the Democratic ticket, and that the Whigs had nominated Jack Hayes, the celebrated Texan ranger. Hayes had been in the Mexican war. It was told of him that when the American and Mexican armies were encamped opposite each other, that a Mexican officer, splendidly equipped, came forward on horseback, and challenged any American to meet him in single combat between the two forces. Jack Hayes volunteered

57

to go, and he killed him. He took his horse, gold watch and personal effects. He afterward learned who he was, and that he left a widow. He sent all his personal effects to her as a present. Of course, we were interested warmly on his side, and he was elected. They say Colonel B. spent all his $80,000 on his side and was defeated.[31] No reputable citizen of San Francisco or business man would allow himself to be seen betting at any of the public gambling tables. He would feel that he was losing character. I am trying to portray the scenes of those days exactly as they occurred, and if I left the gambling scenes out it would not be a true history.

At first public offices went a begging; nobody wanted them. Fine clothes were at a discount. He was looked upon as a tenderfoot who know nothing about the gold regions. But a flannel-shirted, roughly-dressed miner was the lion. He could tell something about the gold regions. The governor appointed a loafer fellow, in the early days, Port Warden. Nobody wanted it, and he was indorsed by one firm. As the city grew very rapidly the office soon became valuable. Somebody told the governor what kind of a man he had appointed Port Warden, and the governor wrote him a letter requesting him to resign, stating to him what representations had been made to him about his character, which, if he had known, he would not have appointed him. He wrote back to the governor refusing to resign, saying to him, he had better read the papers and look after his own character. The governor was up for re-election and the opposition papers were pitching into him.

One warm afternoon my friend Mc and myself thought we would take a walk over to the Presidio; that was about three miles to the Pacific ocean. The seal rocks is where the sea lions or seals can always be seen. It was the entrance to the Golden Gate, where the roar of the Pacific ocean is twice that of the Atlantic, it being six thousand miles broad, twice that of the Atlantic. On our way we stopped into a tent to get a drink of water. We found it occupied by three miners, one of whom was quite lame. I inquired of him what was the matter. He said his hip had been dislocated by the grizzlies. I asked him how it happened. He said they went up to the Trinity river to dig for gold. I knew that was the most remote gold river. He said they were lucky and found rich diggings, but after awhile their provisions gave out and they could not procure any unless they returned to the settlements. On their way, returning on horseback, they came to three grizzly bears grazing in a field. It was very dangerous to attack them, but they were very hungry. They thought if they could kill one of them it would supply them with meat, so they finally decided they would take their chances and fire on them, which they did, and wounded one. The other two took after the man whose hip was dislocated. He fled and came to a buckeye tree, the body of which slants, and he got up on it; the bears came on under it. After awhile they found they could not reach him. It being a low tree one of them commenced climbing it after him. He thought his last hour had come; all the events of his life seemed to rush on his mind, and a picture of the old-fashioned spelling book, where the man plays dead on the bear, came before him, which I distinctly recollected. He thought his only chance was to drop from the tree and hold his breath, and play dead on the bear, which he did, and fell on his face. One bear grabbed him by the shoulders and the other by the ankle, and in pulling, dislocated his hip. He had a thick overcoat on which they tore to pieces. He held his breath. After awhile they went off and left him. He raised his head to see if they were gone, and they came trotting back and smelt him all over again, and went away again, he holding his breath. Then he laid a long time, fearing to move, and his companions came up.

> "Each fainter trace that memory holds
> So darkly of departed years,
> In one broad glance, the soul beholds,
> And all that was at once appears."

In the cases of imminent danger such is said to be the case. It is evident that is what saved this man's life.

The State seal of California is Minerva, with a spear and shield and the grizzly bear at her feet. Before the discovery of gold they were quite numerous. They roamed in full possession, apparently, of the country—no one to molest them or make them afraid. It was a very formidable animal, weighing from seven to eight hundred pounds. When the rainy season set in, late in the fall, and the winter months, during which the grass commenced to grow, he fed on it in the valleys and fields, and became fat and powerful. In the spring, when the dry season set in and no rain for seven months, and fields dried up with a dusty brown, he fled to the tops of the mountains to browse on the leaves of the trees to support life until the next rainy season commenced. It is said he is not a ferocious animal if unmolested, and will not attack you if you let him alone, unless it is a she bear with cubs, or you shoot at them and wound them. They are very hard to kill. To be hit by a bullet has very little effect on them, unless hit in a vital spot. An acquaintance of mine was walking on a road in the interior and saw a big grizzly coming down the road in the opposite direction toward him. He knew it would not do to undertake to run. He had been posted on their natures, so he kept walking right on, as if he was undisturbed and had no fear, the bear coming nearer to him all the time, with his gait unchanged, or he his, until they passed each other, he looking the grizzly in the eye and treating each other with due respect and consideration as friends. As an illustration of their strength, an old Californian informed me that he knew of an instance where a grizzly came into a pack of live mules and took one off and carried it to his den and ate it. In corroboration of that fact, another man informed me that he saw a bear chasing a mule and fired on the bear and hit him, and the bear turned toward him, and the mule escaped.

There was a Mr. W., who opened a fashionable hotel on the east side of the plaza.[32] I was invited to be one of a party of twenty to give a complimentary dinner to a friend, who was about to return East. The bill was just $400, which was $20 apiece, the most I ever paid for a California dinner. The landlord became quite popular and was thought to be a very responsible person. A great many persons from the long voyages around Cape Horn arrived, sick with the scurvy, owing to want of vegetables at sea, most of whose systems underwent a change to become acclimated to the country; some seriously and others more mildly. It was thought it would be a good thing to do to erect a hospital for the benefit of the public and those arriving sick. There was $30,000 raised at the first meeting called, and Mr. W., the landlord, was elected treasurer.

One night he got betting against the game of Faro, lost, and I suppose got over excited, and in trying to recover his losses, lost every thing, including $30,000. Of course it was not known that he ever gambled or he would not have been trusted with the money. As soon as it was known it created great excitement and indignation, that so sacred a fund should have been wasted in that way. He fled, and the Mayor offered $3,000 reward for his apprehension. It seems he had escaped on a vessel to the Sandwich Islands, and had no money, and got in debt there and could not leave there as long as he owed any thing, according to their laws, and he was in despair, until one day fortune smiled upon him. Accidentally he came across a California paper in which was the $3,000 reward offered by the Mayor of San Francisco for his arrest, and this was his opportunity and he seized it at once. Then hope dawned upon him. He found a vessel about to sail for San Francisco. He took the paper and showed it to the captain and told him if he would advance the money so he could pay his debts, he would return with him to San Francisco and he could surrender him and they would divide the reward. The captain accepted his offer and delivered him up upon his arrival at San Francisco, and got the reward. Two or three months had elapsed since his departure, and that was more time than so many years in any other country, and all excitement

61

about it had subsided, and I think it was called a breach of trust, and I have no recollection that he was punished in any other way.[33]

My Blanket Man.

When he wrote me that he had traded the blankets for flour, and had gone to the Yuba river with the flour, I knew that it was a lie, and that he was a rascal, and I found that blankets had been in great demand, at a high price, and likewise learned that he had been connected with a forgery in New York city, but that his brother was a respectable merchant there, so for the time I gave up my $800 as lost. What was my surprise after six weeks at my hotel (which was an expensive one), to see my man at the tea table. I greeted him most cordially and asked no questions about the blankets, but talked to him about the brig I owned and had running to Stockton; that I had been looking for him to come back; there was such a splendid chance for us to make purchases in San Francisco, and for him to take them up on my vessel and sell them out in the Southern gold mines, near that place; that what we had lost on the blankets we could more than make up on the first venture, and that there would be big money in that kind of a speculation. We spent the evening together most cordially. The next morning I detained him in conversation until about the time for the Miners' Bank to open, then we went out together. When we got opposite the bank I took out my watch and said to him, that I did not think it was so late. I said I had a note of $800 due there that morning; I asked him if he had the gold dust about him to that amount. He said yes. I said let me have it and I will take up my note. He said there was no place to weigh it. I said yes, here there was a place where I was acquainted. It was weighed and handed to me. I told him I would see him at dinner, which I did. I then opened on him, and told him how despicably he had acted when I was so generously trusted to his honor. He made no reply; he virtually admitted the truth of my statement. I never saw him afterward. That was the only time I ever played the confidence game in my life, and my conscience has approved of it ever since.

My friend, Mr. R., had got his brewery well under way in Happy Valley, as they called that part of the city, had used up his $8,000 and commenced borrowing money on my endorsement, at ten per cent a month, the regular interest at that time. He had a friend, Lieutenant S., who resigned from the regular army, a graduate from West Point, who had been up in the country, and came back with a flaming account of a place on the Tuolumne river, which empties into the San Joaquin, which was the head of navigation on that river, and was the place to start a town, and if we would furnish him with $1,500 to do it with, we would each own a third of it. I did not take to it, but Mr. R. was so earnest about it, and had such confidence in his friend, that I finally let him have the money. There was quite a spirit of speculation of that kind at that time. Colonel Stevenson had laid out one on Suisan bay, at the mouth of the San Joaquin river, named New York of the Pacific. Marysville, on the Sacramento river, was laid out a short time previous, and proved a great success, making the fortunes of the projectors. Of course, a few were successful, and many failed. It seemed to have been a legitimate thing to do to make a fortune in a new country. I became acquainted with Broderick. It was Kohler & Broderick.[34] They had an office in the same building with Colonel Stevenson. Broderick, who was afterward United States Senator from California, and I became very intimate. He was not intellectually a very brilliant man, but a solid, able and strictly honest man, and a thoroughly posted politician of his day. He had run as a Democratic candidate for Congress from the city of New York, but was not elected. In California he was first elected to the State Senate from the city. It was he who conceived the project of laying out the water lots on the bay, and got the bill through the Legislature. He advised me to buy one or more. I looked at where he suggested to me to buy, and found them six feet under water. Although they could be bought very cheap then, their prospective value seemed so remote to me I thought they were not worth the trouble of bothering with. It shows how easy it is to be mistaken in apprehending the future. I understand they are now the most valuable part of the city.

THE MAN IN HIS TENT.

The man in his tent, who had squatted on Rincon Point, an elevated locality, that commanded a grand view of the bay, informed me that when he squatted there with his tent, that he could find no person who claimed the land. He had been there but a few days, when some parties came to him and offered to give him so much a month for the privilege of putting up their tent near his. He said he had no objections. They paid him. Then other parties who wanted to put up their tents were referred to him. From these various persons he was getting a very liberal income. He informed me that as long as it lasted, he was in no hurry to go to the mines.

ABOUT THIS TIME was the first appearance of the celebrated clipper ships. They anchored off of Happy Valley and attracted great attention; they could make the trip around Cape Horn from New York to San Francisco in three or four months; they run wet; their bows were very sharp, and, in a rough sea, instead of mounting the waves, they cut them, and the bows ran under water, and their progress was not impeded by the waves, saving two or three months' time, which was of great consideration then. There was no railroad across the Isthmus then, and there was no other way of transporting freight between the cities of New York and San Francisco except around Cape Horn. They had great fame then. England conceded their superiority over all other sailing vessels for speed; but they have passed away, the railroad reducing the time to from five to eight days; of course, there is a great difference between that and three or four months. The days of sailing vessels, however great their speed, to a great extent, is gone. Besides, there are regular lines

The Jenny Lind Theatre.

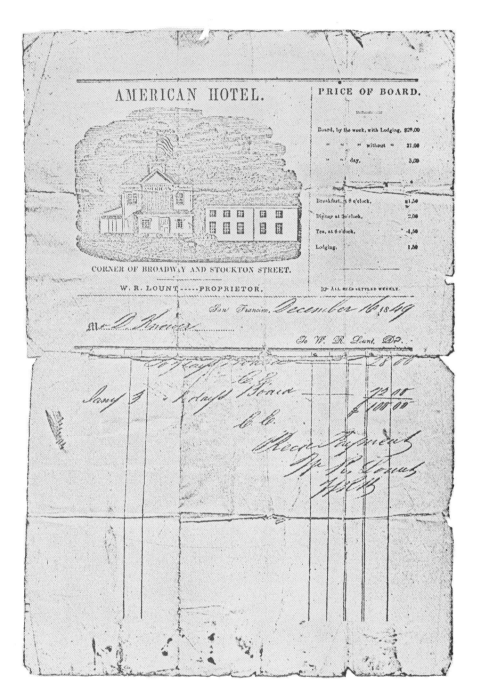

A Bill for Room and Board.

of steamers to most every port of the world, and the ocean is covered with tramp steamers.

That winter a convention was called to organize a State government and apply for admission to the Union.[35] The Southern element there wanted to make it a slave State. The Northerners, including both Whigs and Democrats, wanted it free. They did not want to be brought in competition with slave labor in the mines, and have their occupation degraded in that way. Their pride, as well as interest, was at stake, and there was great feeling on the subject. Meetings were called all through the mines and addresses made and candidates nominated. The average of intelligence there was away above any other part of the country. For they were men of enterprise, or they would not have been there in that early day. At Mormon Island, one of the miners got up and made a speech. He so impressed them with his ability that they unanimously nominated him as their candidate to the Constitutional Convention. He was an old acquaintance of mine. In 1847 or 1848 he was a Democratic member of the Legislature of the State of New York, from Washington county, and was chosen by that body to deliver the oration on Washington's birthday. His name was Winfield S. Sherwood. He was elected to the Constitutional Convention of California, and wrote its first Constitution, copied after that of his native State, New York.[36] The Northern element prevailed in that convention, and California came in a free State by its unanimous vote. Broderick headed the Northern sentiment; Gwin, who had been a United States Marshal in Mississippi, the Southern. I met him often. He would come into a bar-room and say: "I did not come here to dig gold, but to represent you in the United States Senate." He would then say: "Come up all, and take a drink." I thought that was a strange way to inspire the people with the idea that he was the proper person to represent them in the United States Senate. He was elected, with Colonel Frémont, the first two United States Senators from California. At the next election for United States Senators, Broderick got absolute control, and although

65

Gwin had fought him bitterly, they were the two senators to be elected again. Broderick had the magnanimity to induce his friends to go for Gwin and had him elected with him, and Gwin showed his ingratitude by going at once to Washington and securing from Buchanan the control of all the appointments of the government in the State of California.[37] So when Broderick came there, there were none to give his friends. Gwin was afterward very prominent in the rebellion. He went out in a boat in Charleston harbor, crying out from it his advice to Major Anderson, advising him to surrender at the time of the attack on Fort Sumter. (This is a matter of history that occurred after the time of which I am writing.)

A BULL FIGHT.

There were bills posted about the city that three of the most celebrated fighters of Mexico would have an exhibition in the evening, and combat with animals. As my friend and myself never had seen one we thought we would go. It was an amphitheatre, with circular seats about the pit, with thick planks around it, the seats commencing about twenty feet from the bottom of the pit. There was a door at the side of the pit, which was raised by pulleys, which admitted the bull. They were wild ones. Our seat was about the fifth row back. The house was crowded and brilliantly illuminated. Then the bull-fighters were in the pit, one on horseback, two on foot, gorgeously and brilliantly dressed, with swords, the blades pointed like spears, with red flags in their hands to attract the bull. The door was raised and the animal came rushing in; he was a terrible one to look at. Blinded by the lights and the scene, he rushed and roared around the arena; I trembled in my seat, although I was in no possible danger. The first feat of the bull-fighters was to plant a rosette on the shoulders of the animal with a barb implanted in his flesh, which enraged him more, with colored ribbons, two or three feet in length, attached to the rosette, which was flying in the air as he went around, indicating to the audience the success of the feat.

Then the same feat was performed on the other shoulder. Then when the bull attacked the man again, a rosette was implanted between his horns, and the man escaped, which was the most difficult of all. They had red flags in one hand to enrage and blind him, but this bull, he became so furious and enraged that they could not master him. He rushed upon the man on horseback, threw the horse and rider, and, with his horns, tore the entrails out of the horse and killed it. The man was wounded, but escaped. The rest of the fighters fled, and one climbed up the side of the paling and came within two inches of being impaled alive against the side by the bull's horns.

As I write I can, in imagination, hear the sound of the animal's horns as they struck the boards in missing the man. The bull was master of the situation; he had cleared the ring. It was a terrible sight as he roared around in his fury. Then the most startling event of all occurred. It seems incredible, but it is the truth of history, and I must write it.

A greaser, with no weapon, but simply his *seraper,* a shawl that he wore around his shoulders, took that off and stretching it out in his hands, jumped down into the pit of the ring alone, to the entire astonishment of the audience, looked Mr. Bull in the eyes and dodged him with his shawl as the animal attacked him. He had probably been brought up among wild bulls. The audience all arose in excitement, expecting to see him torn to pieces, and crying out for him to escape. The professional bull-fighters got their red flags and drew the bull off, and the greaser escaped, and seemed to be surprised at the excitement of the audience. They succeeded in getting the bull out, and dragging out the dead horse, and letting in a less ferocious one. The same performance was gone through with him, as already described, except that this one was conquered. At last, when the bull pitched at the man, he holds his sword in such a way that the weight of the animal comes on it, and passes between his foreshoulders and penetrates his heart. In an instant the back wilts and the animal lies dead. It was the most sudden change, from full vitality to death; it startled you. It's a shock to your nervous system. My friend and myself said it was the first and last bull-fight we would ever see.

T HE PRICE OF lumber and vegetables kept up. I paid forty cents a pound for potatoes in buying provisions for the hands on my brig. I furnished them enough to last them on the up trip, but not for the return, so they would hurry back. It was now time for the vessel with the houses to arrive, and I expected to buy a ship with the money, and to go to the Sandwich Islands and make, what I considered, a fortune for me, but alas! no *Prince de Joinville* came. It was hope deferred. Finally the rainy season set in in full blast, and all consumption of lumber stopped. The high price had stimulated shipments from everywhere. There was a big reaction in the price.[38] The first prominent failure in the city took place. I think it was Ward & Co., commission merchants and private bankers.[39] It was said it was owing to his large orders of shipments of lumber to that market. He shot himself with a pistol in the morning in his bedroom and died, knowing that he could not meet his creditors if he went to his place of business. About this time it was announced from Telegraph Hill that my vessel, with the houses, was entering the port two or three months after she was due, striking a glutted market. I had four or five thousand dollars to raise to pay the freight on them to get possession of them, or I would lose the capital invested. So instead of making $18,000 profit, which I might have made if they had come on time, I was running the risk of losing the capital invested in them. Colonel Stevenson had selected six of them some time before, which he wanted for his New York of the Pacific, which he said he would make me an offer on as soon as they arrived. I saw it was my only chance to save myself to close that sale. I was at his office in the morning as soon as there was any probability of they being there. I said to him: "The houses have arrived. I am ready to receive your offer for the six you selected." He said he had no money now. I said I did not want any (which was a white lie). I said I would take a draft on Prosper, Whetmore & Co., of New York city, for $3,000, payable in ninety days, and his note for the balance, on his own time. He looked over the plan of the houses again. He said he would not give but so much. I said to him, that was not the question, what will you give? He said I will give you that amount, naming the sum. I said at once, they are sold, they are yours. He gave me the draft on Whetmore & Co., for $3,000, payable in ninety days. Just at this time, his partner, Dr. Parker, came in. The colonel informed him he had bought six of my houses. He said, you have made a mistake. Lumber is in a glutted market. It is falling rapidly. The colonel said, that makes no difference now, I have bought them. The colonel was considered rich. No one there questioned the soundness of his draft. I went with it to all the brokers in the city, but could get no offer for it. I then went to Charley Minton, the agent of the steamer *Senator*. I thought he could send it to New York to the owners of the steamer for its face value. He said, the best he could do with me was to give me $2,250 for it. Money was ten percent a month, and scarce at that. Three months time, at the rate of interest there, would be $900. I said, I would take it. He gave me a check on his broker for that amount. He paid me in gold, $16 Spanish doubloon pieces. I tied them up in my handkerchief, and went to Macondray & Co., and said to him, the vessel, with my houses, I see, are consigned to you. I will pay you $2,000 now on the freight, and before they are all taken off the ship, I will pay you the balance. He said, take them all off, and pay the balance at your convenience (we were acquainted and had come up on the same steamer and played whist together). It cost me $800 to get them ashore. There were no wharves then. They had to be taken ashore on lighters. I expected my brig down from Stockton soon, with $2,000 freight money, so I was out of the woods financially for the present. I then made arrangement with the colonel to have them landed on the North Beach on land owned by him, where I could retail out my other six houses, which I had to sell, when I got a proper price for them. We formed a copartnership. I was to take one of my smallest houses, and have it erected there, to be used for an office, and to use the grounds as a lumber yard to sell on commission, and as a place for storage, which was very scarce then. There were quite a number who had taken the liberty of piling lumber and other articles on it, using it as public ground. I took formal possession of it in the name of Colonel Stevenson, and gave notice to the different parties that if they did not remove their materials from the premises in ten days they would be charged so much for storage. Some removed, and others did not. I recollect the German house that did not remove it in thirty days after the ten days of notice. It was a wealthy house, and I handed them a bill of $250 for storage, at which they demurred very seriously, questioning our title; but they paid it. When I went out to the ship to see about taking my houses off, I met the first mate, whom I got acquainted with in New York. I told him I thought the ship had been lost; that all the old tugs had got in ahead of them. He said to me, I have had the worst time I ever had in my life. I have had to carry that old man on my shoulders (referring to the captain) all the way. Whenever we had a good breeze and sails were all full, he would come on deck and order shorten sail to check our speed, or we might have been here a month sooner. That told the whole story. I saw them take freight, in my presence, when they were offered $1.50 per foot, when they told me there was no room for the other half of my houses to go on the ship, when I had a legal contract with them at sixty cents per foot. My freight alone would have made a difference of two or three thousand dollars by excluding it and taking the other in at the difference in the price of it. There is no doubt they served many other shippers and put their goods on other vessels, and kept theirs back until the other ships would get to San Francisco ahead of them, so that they could deliver the freight according to their bills of lading on the arrival of the *Prince de Joinville*. That was why my speculation was ruined by their dishonesty. Instead of being the fastest ship, it was a fraud, a decoy, a dead trap on those who were unfortunate enough to ship by it. When I saw the captain he was very humble. He had all kinds of apologies to make, and invited me to go to China with him. I could have the best stateroom on his ship. It should not cost me a dollar. I could go around the world with him. I saw that my speculation was ruined by their dishonesty, and there was no remedy, and, like all human events, that ended it, and I had to abandon my Sandwich Island expedition and throw my anticipated fortune from it to the winds. Mr. Meiggs, the one who failed and ran away to Chile, and built the railroad in that country from Valparaiso to its capital, and then organized a company and constructed railroads in Peru, had a lumber yard side of me.[40] I sold, after a while, my other six houses, one at a time, retailing them out, and, by careful management, just succeeded in saving my original capital.

I was satisfied with San Francisco, with my interest in the lumber yards, and with my partnership with Colonel Stevenson on the North Beach. My interest in my brig, when it came down, and my prospective interest in what was to be the city of Tuolumne, and my associations with Mr. R., who was building the first brewery on the Pacific, which I was backing up with my indorsement, and I was to have one-third interest when it was completed, if I wanted it, at first cost, looked like a very favorable investment for me at that time. I was living an active and enterprising life, with bright hopes of future fortune. One morning when I went down to the North Beach I found there had been a house erected on our land in the night. I, of course, informed the colonel at once. He informed me it was a man by the name of Colton, who pretended to have a title under what he called the "Colton Grant," and that it was bogus, and that he had the building erected to try and force his title.[41] The colonel said he would see the judge of the court in the city, and get an order for its removal. In about two hours he sent a messenger with an order from the judge authorizing us to remove it. He instructed me to employ all the men that were necessary, and have the material removed from the premises and he would pay the bill, which I did, and our title was not disputed after that.

I had never been on a trip to Stockton, and I had chartered the freight capacity of the brig to a man for $1,800. He was to put in it all the freight he chose to. I thought it would not be for his interest to overload it. If the vessel sunk there was no insurance —his cargo would be a total loss. I had reserved the deck and the passenger room. The conditions of the charter were that the freight was to be delivered in Stockton by a certain date or I was to forfeit the $1,800. The freight was aboard; he had loaded the vessel deeper than I had expected. I had a number of passengers at $15 each. They were to furnish their own provisions, but to have the privileges of the cooking stove on deck. The vessel was anchored out in the bay, to sail at 2 P. M., when the tide was most favorable. I had a new chain for the anchor, and the captain said he wanted a kedge anchor for safety, so I ordered one from Macondray & Co., for $35, on condition that, without fail, they would have it on board before 2 P. M. We were all on board by 1 o'clock, waiting for the favorable tide, to start. At 1:30 no anchor and the bay was very rough. The captain said it would not come, they would not venture out in that sea in a small boat. I said it would be there certain, I knew my man. Sure enough, in a few moments we could just see a boat in the distance, two men rowing and one guiding the rudder. They came alongside and we had the anchor aboard in five minutes. In the stern was Mr. Watson, one of the firm. He said he was afraid to trust his men in that sea for fear they would fail to deliver it. The profit on it to them was only $3.50, and it was a very wealthy firm, but they had pledged their word to me that they would have it there at that time. (Would that there were more of such honorable men). We hoisted anchor, the tide in our favor and a stiff breeze blowing. We passed out of the bay of San Francisco into San Pablo Bay, and crossed that into the Straits of Benica, which is four miles long and connects with Suisun bay. The Straits of

Benicia was a perfectly safe anchorage. It was approaching night, and blowing almost a gale. I was in hopes and expected that the captain would come to anchor in the straits and wait until morning before venturing out into the Suisun bay, which was twenty miles across to the mouth of the San Joaquin river, where we were bound. The bay was almost like the open sea; you could get out of sight of land. I think he would have come to anchor if I, the owner, had not been on board, and had not urged upon him the importance of having the vessel in Stockton in time. As he was the captain I felt sensitive about interfering with his business, and had hoped and expected, all the way through the straits, that he would come to anchor, and not undertake to cross the bay that night. Darkness was setting in, but he did not come to anchor. The gale increased to a hurricane; all sails were taken in, and we were scudding under bare poles, and had a lantern hung up in the rigging. The captain came to me and said, loaded as we were, we could not live in that gale; he would have to seek a place to anchor on the side of the bay. I said to him, he was the captain. The line was thrown out every few minutes. At last we found sounding, and the anchor was cast. We had been there but a short time before another vessel, more than twice as large as ours, came aside of us, with a heavy deck-load of lumber, and got entangled in our anchor chain, and kept drawing us nearer to them. If they had struck our vessel we knew we were lost. They would have sunk us at once. Seven times they came down on us and each time, by superhuman efforts, we warded the blow, all hands and passengers doing their best, fully realizing the danger they were in. It seems to me that I hear now the oaths of the captain of the other vessel rising above the sounds of the terrific hurricane as he was ordering his men, for they, too, were in danger if they collided with us. Of course, he was on the bare poles. As he came on us the eighth time they hoisted their jib sail. As the wind struck it, it seemed to lift their vessel out of the water, and, thank God, we were freed from it. It was forty-five years ago, and, as I write it, all lives before me as visible

73

as if it were yesterday. The captain of the other vessel had seen our light, and, supposing we were in the right channel, had followed us. We had escaped what seemed almost certain death, but were not out of danger. Our new good chain was attached to our bad chain, and the captain had let out all our chain to free us from the other vessel, so we were actually hanging by our bad chain in the open roadstead, not in the protection of a harbor, and liable to drag our anchor or break our chain and be wrecked; but we could do nothing more than submit to our fate. I thought I would get into my berth and try and get some sleep, and, if I found myself alive in the morning, we might be saved. I did sleep, and when I awoke it was daylight. The gale was subsiding. We had dragged our anchor. The bow of our brig was very sharp; the banks were soft mud, and we had struck it with such force that we were wedged in. The tide was low and we were almost out of water. We fortunately had struck the land with our bow, and that was what saved us. If we had struck with the side of the vessel we would have been wrecked. So, ever since we had been freed from the other vessel, we had been in safety and did not know it. We waited for the tide to rise and then got our kedge anchor out and pulled the vessel out off the bank as the tide rose. The sea was very rough, but the gale had subsided, and by 11 o'clock we were entering the mouth of the San Joaquin river in safety. It was forty miles up the river to Stockton. The river was in a valley of Tulares. The land seemed to be in the course of formation. There was but one tree between the mouth and Stockton, a willow, called the Lone Tree. The only place on its banks where the soil had formed solid enough to produce one, surrounded by hills at that season of the year, covered with beautiful wild flowers. The scenery was magnificent. As the river curved we could see the white sails of other vessels. They looked as if they were in a field. You could not see the water at a little distance, the river being narrow. We could almost jump from our deck to the banks. We felt in perfect safety. Contrasting that with the night before in that terrible hurricane and in the death struggles for our lives, it produced a supreme feeling of ethereal ideal happiness that this earth seemed almost a Paradise. The captain informed me that there was one place on the river where we might have to anchor. It was called Devil's Elbow. There was a sharp turn in the river and the current was rapid, and we might have to pull the vessel around it; but sometimes, if it was favorable, he could sail around it, and if done successfully, then the vessels that had come to anchor could find no fault; otherwise you had to come to behind the others and take your turn. When we were coming to it, he was at the helm and I at his side, to see what was the best to do. As we approached, we saw several vessels had come to for the purpose of pulling around. The last was a large vessel that the captain said could never get around. If we anchored behind it we might not be able to deliver our freight according to the charter. We had put an English sailor in the hold to let the anchor go, in case we did not succeed, if we gave him the signal to do so. As we came to the place with all sails set, there was a breeze sprung up, filling all the sails. I said to the captain, let her go. As we passed the vessels that had come to anchor there was a howling and yelling from them of derision and anger at us for going by them. Just as we got two-thirds of the way around, the sailor in the hold let the anchor go without orders. He got frightened. If he had not, we would have made it successfully. As it was, we got ahead of all the other vessels, and got to Stockton in ample time. The next morning there was a drove of mules at the side of the brig, and the cargo was being discharged and packed on their backs to be taken to the mining camps, as there were no good roads there in those early days. About all the grain and flour came from Valparaiso and Chile, put up very nicely in fifty and one hundred pound sacks, so it was easy to handle. As soon as all the mules were packed, the head mule, who had on a bell fastened around his neck, which rang as he went, was started first, and all the rest, in single file, followed him, and they were going for the different mining camps in the interior. In two or three days we were unloaded, and we were prepared to return. The freight money was paid to me in gold, at $16 per ounce in full, all being satisfactory to the shipper. I had delivered it within the time specified. One of the passengers who came up with me, a tailor, from Salem, Mass., asked me if I would not give him a free passage back on the vessel to San Francisco; that he wanted to try to get home; he was discouraged. I said to him you have traveled eighteen thousand miles to get to the gold mines, and now you are within half a day of them and want to go home without trying your fortune. If you do go, you will never forgive yourself, but go to the mines and try your luck; then if you are discouraged and want to go back, I will give you a free passage, as we have no passengers on our return trip.

Home Sickness.

When a person was attacked with it, it seemed the worst kind of malady, as it would take months to return if they had the money to pay their passage. Many were married men, separated a great distance from their wives and children. Others, young men, who had their engaged ones waiting for them to return, with their fortunes made in the gold mines, to marry them. I can recall several instances where I have known them to lie down and die from despair. I was talking with an old Californian of those days. He said he had once given up and made up his mind to wander off by himself on the mountains and die, which he did. As he lay there in despair, after a while he thought he would look around him, and he saw the hill was covered with a variety of beautiful wild flowers. He said their beauty seemed to refresh and revive his mind, and give him new resolution, and he decided to try his fortune again, and he became successful and returned to the States with a competency.

THE EARLY PIONEERS had some conflict with the Indians in the interior of the country. Five Oregon men were massacred by them when engaged in digging gold, but a terrible retribution was visited upon those Indians concerned in it by the enraged Forty-niners. The Indians, at first had nothing but bows and arrows, and, of course, could not compete with rifles. Several other small engagements were rumored, but they soon gave up all contests with the whites, for they saw it was useless. There was an acorn that was quite plenty in California, being longer than ours, but not of a bitter taste. The squaws made flour of them. The Digger Indians were the next tribe east of them; they were probably the lowest grade. They would set fire to the prairie grass to burn the grasshoppers, and pick them up and eat them. They deemed them a luxury. The Oregon tribes were a higher grade, a warlike race, and superior in every respect. The highest grade of them, in the United States now, are the Choctaws and Chicksaws that formerly occupied the northern parts of the State of Mississippi. When a young man, I spent three weeks in their nation, traveling alone, and was treated with great hospitality by them. They are quite intelligent, and they have laws and customs as civilized nations. We generally look upon all of them as alike, but such is not the case—there is as great a difference between different tribes as much as between different white nations. The California Indians were not naturally warlike, and when the early pioneers expected any trouble from them, they would appoint a committee to go and see them, and they generally settled their difficulty without any conflicts.

There were about sixteen Jesuit missionary stations in the country before the discovery of gold, and were there for the purpose of converting the Indians to the Catholic church, and when converted, generally made them work to sustain their missionary establishments.[42]

I had returned to my office on the North Beach after my only trip to Stockton on my brig. My friend R. was progressing with his brewery. He had received a favorable letter from Lieutenant S. about our Tuolumne city, and informing me that S. had a diamond ring that cost $800 in Rio Janeiro, at a broker's office, as collateral security for $250 borrowed on it at ten per cent per month, and the time was about up. If I would redeem the ring I could keep it and wear it until he paid me. I went and saw the ring. It was as represented, and I redeemed it and wore it for a considerable time. One day R. came to me with a flaming letter from S. that he had laid out the city and been elected alcalde, and we would make our fortune, and there was a friend of S. that was going up there, and if I would send up the ring by him he would appreciate it so much, and he would be responsible that I should not lose any thing by it. I was foolish enough to be persuaded by him and handed him the ring, for which act I have never forgiven myself. That was the last I ever saw of the ring or any of the money invested in Tuolumne city, for it turned out a failure. It was never the head of navigation on the river, or any thing else that was ever heard of.[43]

There were three unfortunate events that occurred in California in the winter months of 1849 and the beginning of 1850. The rainy season had destroyed all the dams constructed on the gold rivers and raceways, which had been constructed at great expense for the purpose of working the beds of the river for gold, the rivers often rising from ten to eighteen feet in a night, and the current running with terrible force. The second, the flooding of Sacramento, destroying large quantities of merchandise and carrying away and undermining the houses there. The third was the great fire in San Francisco, destroying one-third of the main business portion of the city, upon which there was no insurance. There were no companies organized or agents there to insure property then, as it was too risky. There was one four-story fire-proof building that was stored full of the most valuable goods, at a large price for storage, for it was considered absolutely fire-proof, but when the fire came the heat of the fire from the buildings around it caused the iron sides of it to expand, which let the roof fall in and burned everything to the ground, so that nothing was saved. Instead of being a place of safety, it was the most destructive of all.[44]

Some ships in the bay were burned. I succeeded in getting in the rear of the fire to save my brig. I ordered the men to hoist anchor and put out further in the bay, which saved it. These unfortunate events destroyed and marred the fortune of many. On the day before I called on a private banker, G., on the plaza, and presented my check for $800.[45] He said to me, if it made no difference, it being steamer day (once a month they went East when the gold was shipped to the mint in Philadelphia by them), and if I would call in the morning for it, it would be an accommodation to him. I said I wanted to use it. He commenced weighing it out. I then thought it would make no difference to me and it was mean not to accommodate him, for I might want some favor of him. I said, if I can have it in three days without fail it would answer my purpose. He said, you can have it now, pouring the gold in the scales to weigh it. I said never mind, I don't want it now. The fire came that night, burnt his place up and all his property. He was a ruined man. I never saw him afterward.

Mr. G., to whom I had bargained to sell my houses to arrive, (and he backed out) was an Englishman from Liverpool. He had about all the consignments of shipments from that city (evidently being very popular there), to sell on commission at ten per cent; when the goods came and were sold, instead of remitting the capital to the owners and being satisfied with his commission, he used it in buying property and in erecting buildings in San Francisco. He had constructed a fire-proof building which he rented to the government for a post-office, at a large sum per month, likewise the first theatre in the city, and other buildings. He informed me at one time how much his rents amounted to per month; the sum was several thousand dollars. Money was worth but three to five percent in England per year to the owners of the merchandise; while in California it was in demand at ten per cent per month. I suppose he thought he would make a great fortune for himself and then return to England (where he had a wife and children) and pay up all his obligations with extra allowance, for the use of the money, and make all satisfactory; but the great fire destroyed all his buildings, and he was a ruined man, there being no insurance in the city then. I met a friend in New York about two years after my return from California; I asked him when he saw Mr. G. last. He said, "it was about 11 o'clock one day at a hotel where he invited some friends to take a drink. Mr. G. was there, he declined; but afterward called him to one side and asked him to loan him $1, saying he had had no breakfast that morning." Such was an example of the fluctuations of fortune in those days.

Some parties came with various kinds of machinery that was to make a certain fortune for them, and was taken up into the interior at great expense. I never knew of one that was successful. About all the companies that were formed in the States to go around Cape Horn for mining purposes generally dissolved after arriving in California, but what they brought with them for supplies, sold for so high a price that it generally sold for more than the cost of their passage, and they had money coming to them. Some companies bought the ships as they came in and hired the captain. I recollect one, called the *Mechanics' Own*. Every person joining their company in the States had to be voted in and pay $1,000. They put on airs and talked quite aristocratic of their captain as their boy.

Three persons started the first bank in San Francisco, called the Miners' Bank, on the northwestern corner of the plaza. Mr. Haight, who was from Rochester, N.Y., and the sutler of Colonel Stevenson's regiment, was one of them. It was said that at first they bought gold as low as $8 per ounce, when it was worth more than $18 at the mint East. The owners of the bank made $100,000 each in three or four years.

Before the discovery of gold the then small places on the Pacific Coast obtained their supplies from small trading vessels that sailed along the coast and stopped at their towns occasionally. After the discovery of gold, at first goods went up four or five times their previous value, and when one of these vessels

Just Received—a Shipment of Fine Segars.

A Patron of the Arts.

was seen entering the port, parties would put out in small boats to get aboard of them before they came to anchor (they on board knowing nothing about the discovery of the gold), would bargain with them for some of their goods, and finally offer them so much for all their cargo. It being beyond their expectations the offer was generally accepted, and thus some big speculations were made.

A lieutenant of Stevenson's regiment, who had been down in Monterey and had not heard of the gold discovery, on his first day in San Francisco, informed me that he did not know what to make of things. Most of his old acquaintances wanted to know if he did not want to borrow some money; they had some that he could have as well as not.

The steamers came in once a month with letters and papers. The long lines were formed to the post-office. Sometimes it took half a day to get there. The New York papers at first sold for $1 each. Then they got down to fifty cents. I sold the *New York Herald,* that was more than a month old, that contained the latest news there from the States in the interior, for $5, and the man coaxed it out of me at that, for I wanted to give it to a party of friends I was going to see in the mining districts. I knew it would be a great treat to them. It is almost impossible to recall all the exact scenes of those days, so as to have them fully realized by the reader.

The city of San Francisco was extending more rapidly in what they called the Happy Valley district, which was toward the Mission of Dolores, established by the Jesuits.⁴⁶ I visited it when the building was intact. I recollect a painting of an Indian warrior, with his bows and arrows, the implements of war, represented as a saint ascending to heaven—I suppose to create favorable impression on Indians and make converts of them.

My friend was going on with his brewery, and borrowing money and getting me deeper on his paper. He heard that I had $2,500 deposited with Macondray & Co., and pleaded with me to let him have it as it would carry him through. I had lost all confidence in him, and felt it would be like throwing it in the sea. I informed him that I had shipped it the day before, which I had not, but went right down and gave an order for its shipment, for fear he might over-persuade me to let him have it, and I thus saved it. When most completed, a barrel of alcohol that was in the building bursted, and it ran down to the furnace and set it on fire, and burnt it up. That was the fate of the first brewery started in California. Since then there have been millions made in that business there."

The North Beach property, after I had sold all my houses out, I closed my interest in. It proved a failure to use for a wharf or shipping point.

During the seven months of summer the northwest wind blew there so hard every afternoon that it was not a safe place for vessels, and the property would never have any value for that purpose, and I do not think it has ever been used since for that.

In the winter months, which is generally the rainy season, the wind blows from the south for five months, and the other seven months it blows from the north-west over six thousand miles of ocean, and consequently, is not impregnated with any decayed vegetable matter, and is as pure as air can be. In San Francisco the sun would rise in a clear sky every morning and there would be a perfect calm; by 11 A. M. there would be a little breeze; by 2 or 3 o'clock, a gale. When the sun set the wind would subside and there would be a perfect calm again. Every day would be the same, month after month. What was almost a gale on the coast would be a gentle breeze up in the mining district, in the interior. The next day that air would be displaced by another gale from over the thousand miles of ocean, for it is impossible to imagine any other country with purer air.

During that time there were various visionary reports of new discoveries of gold regions, one of a lake that the sands of its banks were rich with gold. All you had to do, to make your fortune, was to wash it out, which produced quite a sensation, and parties were organized to go there, but they never found it. The next year after the purchase of my brig, there were small steamers constructed to run to Stockton, and they had already some sailing vessels put on, built there, and the price of freight had commenced falling, and I thought I had better sell my vessel while I could get a good price for it. There was a man who came to me and said he wanted to buy it; that he had been a captain of a boat on Lake Erie. I stated to him my price for it. He said that was not out of the way, but he would like to try it one trip before closing the purchase, and referred me to a mercantile house there as his reference. They said he had run vessels for them on Lake Erie when they were doing business in Buffalo. I concluded that was entirely satisfactory; that that had evidently been his regular business. He said he wanted to employ all his own hands. I had the vessel, at the time, half loaded with freight, which I turned over to him. I paid my men and discharged them, and told them the vessel was about to change owners, and put him in full possession of it. Of course I had nothing more to do with it until he returned from the trip to Stockton; then I expected he would close the purchase as he said that the price was satisfactory to him. After a few weeks I commenced looking for the return of my brig, but it did not come. Finally I heard a rumor that the captain had left the vessel at Stockton, but did not believe it, but thought that some accident might have happened. I had borrowed a spy-glass to investigate the bay. I could have recognized my vessel by the red streak around it. Finally, after it had been gone long enough to make several trips, I discovered it at anchor in the bay. I went and supplied myself with money, in case it should prove true that the captain had left the vessel, to pay his men in full before they got ashore, because the vessel was liable for their wages, whoever might have employed them; so I hired a boat to row me out to it. I met a man on the deck that seemed to be in command. I inquired of him where the captain was. He said he had run away. I spoke to him in a sharp tone of voice and said, how do you know that? He said, because I saw him on the back of a mule going over the plain. Then he asked me, are you the owner? I said, yes. Then I said, you have all got your pay before he went; I did not employ you. He said, some of them have got some.

As you seem to be in command, I suppose you have kept an account of how it stands. He said, "Come down in the cabin and I will show it to you." I said, "It was hard on me to be robbed of all my freight money, but it was also hard for them to be cheated out of their hard earnings, and I would see what I could do for them." He presented the statement of what each man had received and what was due them. I was surprised at his correctness. I said: It seems all right and I would pay them, which I did, and took their receipt. I was afraid if they went ashore and found the vessel was liable for their wages they might make any kind of demands, so I got possession of my vessel again, very much damaged. Before leaving the port he had let the steamer *Senator* run into the bows of the vessel, and it cost me $700 to have it repaired, ships carpenters' wages being $20 per day, payable in gold. The events which I had anticipated of the decline of that kind of property had come, and, after it was repaired, I put it up at auction and sold it, so that rascal cost me several thousand dollars.

HAVING SOME LEISURE I thought I would take a trip up the mining regions, and make a visit to my old friends there. More than a year had passed, and greater changes had taken place than would have occurred in any other country in many years. The population of California increased one hundred thousand the first year after the discovery of the gold, which had accounted for the great changes which had taken place since my previous trip. I went up on the steamer *Senator* to Sacramento, which had become quite a city, and the next morning started for Coloma in a stage full of passengers, drawn by mules. I took a seat aside of the driver. I got in conversation with the driver. I asked him what pay he received? He said, only $450 per month and his board. I asked him if he had driven stages before? He said, yes, out of Boston. I said, at what wages? He said, $14 a month. I said that there was a big difference between that and $450. He said, yes, but that this was his last trip. He took a party of three up only a few weeks ago, and he brought them down yesterday, and they had between $3,000 and $4,000 apiece, and he was not going to waste his time driving for $450 a month. He was going to the mines the next day. It was quite probable that the party referred to had made an unusual lucky strike, for I had met parties that had done the same thing. I had had in my hands at one time, in San Francisco, a piece of solid gold metal, something in the shape of the cover of a sugar loaf, that was worth $4,500, found by a couple of green Irishmen. They inquired of some miners in the interior where was a good place to dig. The miners said in fun, dig in that sand bank behind you. The Irishmen took them up in earnest and went to digging. In a short time they found that chunk of gold, where no experienced miner would think of digging.

I have dug gold in the cellar of the brewery in San Francisco. I think most all the soil of that part of California is impregnated with gold. But the point is to find it in sufficient quantities to pay to dig it. As an illustration, if you knew that in a certain piece of ground there was $5,000 worth of gold, and it cost you $10,000 to wash all the ground to get it, of course that land would have no gold value. I found at Coloma that my friends had left the Dutch bar and gone to the middle fork of the American river, some distance from there. I got directions how to get there and started on foot. Toward night I met a young man who had just came overland and had separated that day from his party to get work in the mining camp. I told him where I was going, and that he had better go with me, and that he could get from $10 to $16 per day to work for other parties, or to join two others and work a claim for himself, which he did. So as it was getting toward night, we camped under a tree and slept until morning, and took a fresh start. That day we found the middle fork of the American river and my friends. The river was sunk way down in the earth. It seemed almost a mile down to the water where they were to work. It was quite a large mining place. The excitement there every day was when the "dummy" went into the river. It was a diving armor that had been used in the gulf of Lower California to go down in the deep waters to hunt for pearls, and had been brought by a party of five, each putting in $800, making $4,000, expecting to make their fortunes by getting into the deep water of the gold rivers.[48] (As I have shown before, the torrents and force of the currents had prevented any gold from ever lodging there.) Every day at such an hour, it was announced that the "dummy" was a going in the river. The other miners quit their work to see it, and the proprietors of the "dummy" always treated the crowd in the most lavish manner. Its credit was good for any store bills. Its always treating the crowd had made it popular, and nobody would trade with the storekeeper who would not trust it, so it was death to the prosperity of the storekeeper, whether he trusted it or not. They never got any gold while there through "dummy," and when he left to go further down the river to try another place, the main storekeeper there lost $800 by trusting it, which broke him. These stores were tents, to supply immediate wants of the miners. I never heard of "dummy" afterward. I have no doubt he operated on all the store tents until he came to grief like all evil-doers.

The productiveness of the gold rivers had not diminished any that I could perceive. I talked to a man who had been off a little ways to prospect in another place. I asked him what luck? He said, there was nothing there. I said, was there no gold? He said, yes, there was some, but of no value. He said a man could make $10 a day, and who was going to waste their time on that. My visit over, I returned to San Francisco. My friend R.'s brewery was not completed. I was informed he had been borrowing money from a Jew at twenty per cent a month. It was no use for me to back him any more, however valuable it might be, if completed, and I had no doubt there was a fortune in it, but neither he nor I had the capital to do it.

I had some other financial entangling matters, and I was afraid if I kept on with them I might get broke, and the only way I saw of getting out with them was to announce that I was going to leave, and going down to Realejo, Central America.[49]

There was an English steamer advertised to sail for that port and Panama. I thought I would go for sixty days and then return and commence again and manage my affairs in a more conservative way, and what I could control. Well I closed my matters out the best I could and engaged my passage on the steamer for Realejo. There was considerable excitement at this time about the Nicaragua route. The above place would be the terminus on the Pacific coast, and, consequently, a place of importance. As I had missed it in trading six of my houses for lots in San Francisco, there might be a chance to get some there in advance of any rise on them. Any way, I wanted to get out of my entangling alliances and take a fresh start. The night before I sailed Mr. Brady (Colonel Stevenson's son-in-law) came to me and said the colonel did not like to have me go. I told him I had paid my passage, $200. He said the colonel understood that. He put his hand in his vest pocket and pulled out a roll of bills. He said, here is the $200, which he told me to give you, so you will not lose anything by not going. There was once a lady, the wife of one of the officers of his regiment, who arrived there, expecting to meet her husband, but he was up in the country. The colonel asked me to go down to the steamer and meet her, and escort her to a boarding-house to stay until her husband arrived, which I did. I told him that she was short of funds, having expected to meet her husband. He gave me $150 and told me to give it to her, as if I loaned it to her, and when her husband paid me I could return it to him. I mention these little incidents to show that whatever faults he may have had, he was the most generous of friends.

I sailed out of the port of San Francisco on the steamer

Ecuador for Realejo, Central America, expecting to return to California within sixty days.[50] In a few days, out at sea, we began to hear unfavorable rumors about our vessel; that the engineer had left the day before our sailing; that he did not consider it safe to go in it; that it could not carry coal enough to take it to Acapulco, the next coaling place. And we were informed that it was a steamer that had been running from Panama to Valparaiso, and had been brought up by a speculator and sent up to San Francisco as an experiment, to see if it would pay. The officers and men had never been up the coast before, and knew nothing about the port. One day we were startled in mid ocean by the stopping of the engine. We soon found the cause. The captain was about to try his sails so as to save coal (which verified the reports about being short of coal). We made some headway with the sails, but lost it again when the wind subsided, by the currents of the ocean; so that project was abondoned, and after some days we put into the port of San Blas, in Mexico, for fuel. There was no coal there, so we laid in all the wood we could to try and reach Acapulco (here we could not buy any thing with our $5 gold pieces, but they were ready to sell for silver). The cholera had been there, they said, but had left. The priests had had a procession, and, with their incense boxes, had marched through the streets and driven it out. We took in all the wood we could get and started to make the port of Acapulco, the regular coaling port for all the steamers on that coast. It was Sunday P. M. We could raise fuel enough to make only four knots an hour. It was an iron steamer. We were burning what there was of the woodwork of the vessel, for if we could not make the port before dark we were lost. The officers were not acquainted with the coast. We had not fuel enough to keep steam up all night, and we would be on the broad Pacific ocean, six thousand miles across, without the remotest possibility of meeting any other vessel, without any control of our steamer, subject to be driven in any direction. I heard the mate talking to the captain about the propriety of wrecking the vessel and saving what lives they could, although we were in sight of land. The captain said the under-tow was so great that none could be saved in that way. It is twice as great on the Pacific as the Atlantic. There were no female passengers. One man said he had $10,000 in gold with him; if his wife and children only had that he would be content to meet his fate, under the circumstances, but it was hard to leave them without it. All the passengers had more or less gold, or they would not have been returning.

You can imagine with what anxiety we watched every indication of the coast to see if there was any chance of us nearing the port. Finally, toward night, we saw a high projection of land on the coast, and that was predicted that it was the entrance to the port. If we could reach that point before dark, we might be saved. The passengers went to work to break up any thing for the fires that would make steam. The captain made no objections, but told them to burn all woodwork on the vessel to save their lives. At dark we reached the point we had in view, and it was fortunate for us that it was the entrance to the port. As the vessel turned to enter, you could see, coming over the waters of the ocean, a tropical storm, accompanied with wind, thunder and lightning. Twenty minutes later it would have reached us, and we would have been lost. As soon as we got safely in port (and it was very dark), I can hear now, in imagination, the sound of the anchor as it was let down in the water, which assured our entire safety. It thundered and lightninged, and blowing a high gale, which was music to our ears, as we knew we were out of danger, and feeling the supreme gratification of knowing what we had escaped. Blessed to us was the high mountains which surrounded the port. The entrance to it is narrow, but when you get inside it is one of the safest harbors in the world, being perfectly land-locked. The next day opened on a happy lot of passengers. I felt as if I was commencing life anew. We went ashore expecting to be there several days, as they proposed to take in a full supply of coal. This place had been once quite a city, but many years ago had been partly destroyed by an

89

earthquake. It was said that the water went out of the bay most to the tops of the mountains, and then reacted to its usual level in the harbor; that there was a French ship carried up to the sides of the mountains, and when the water reacted, carried back in safety in the harbor. Hundreds of buildings were destroyed, the ruins of which are now visible where the city once extended.

I WAS INTRODUCED TO General Alvarado. He was the most prominent man in Mexico, on the Pacific coast, at that time, and afterward became very prominent in the public affairs of his country. On our return to the vessel that evening there was quite an excitement on board. Among the passengers was a party of three who had been quite successful in Sacramento in the bottling of soda and summer beer, and peddling it out through the city. They had picked up by chance an old acquaintance from Waterford who belonged to an aristocratic family there, and by his habits of dissipation was a mortification to them. So when the California excitement broke out, they furnished him with money to go to the gold regions. It would either reform him or they would get rid of him. Of course, such men were no good in California, and he had spent his money and wanted to return. These men came across him and told him they were going to return East in sixty days, and if he would keep straight, and drive one of their wagons for them, they would take him home with them. When they went ashore the first day they left him in charge of their baggage, and promised him that he could go ashore the next. They had their private store of wines and brandy. He had found it and tried it and got full, and treated all the sailors and everybody on board that would drink with him, and was the most popular man on board with the sailors. He repented the next day and begged their forgiveness, and they took him home with them. Like a bad penny, he returned as he was before. Distance did not reform him.

Well, our next port was Realejo, my destination. Just after dark one day we got opposite to what, according to the charts, was that port. It was necessary for them to wait until morning before they could undertake to enter it, as they had never been there before, and there were no pilots, and they decided not to let the steam go down, and they concluded that they would sail slowly around in a circle, so as to be opposite to the port in the morning. When morning came it was foggy, and we could not see the land. But they had such confidence in the correctness of their chart that they determined to enter it. Instead of port, we came to the white caps, dashing against the rocks almost mountains high, and we came within an ace of being dashed to pieces against them. If the engineer had not reversed the movement of the engine the instant he did, we would have been wrecked. The captain was now completely befogged. In a short time he came to me with a paper to sign agreeing to go to Panama. It should cost me nothing extra for my passage there; that the few other passengers for that port had signed it. I thought I had better sign to go anywhere than to take any more chances in that steamer. Come to find out afterward, instead of being opposite the port that morning, we were twenty miles from it, the currents of the ocean having carried us that distance while we were sailing around in a circle, which they had not ciphered on, and thus came so near wrecking us. By chance we saw a sailing vessel. The captain gave orders for the steamer to follow it, and, when we overtook it, we found it was bound for Realejo. There was a man on board of it who was acquainted with the port. They got him to come on our steamer and had him pilot us to that port, so I expected to go ashore, and got my baggage in readiness, and, when the time came, had it brought up on deck. They did not enter the port, but came to outside. There were two passengers, it seems, that would not sign the paper to go to Panama, and it was to land them he had come to, and when I went to have my baggage put in the small boat the captain informed me I had signed to go to Panama, and some of the other passengers said

91

I was very foolish to risk my life in that sea in so small a boat. Before I scarcely knew it the boat had pushed off without me, and, consequently, the whole current and course of my life was changed. Upon such little incidents often do the events of human life depend. It may have been fortunate for me that I did not land there.

There was in Nicaragua at the time a filibustering expedition under the command of Captain Walker, who went from California to overthrow the government there by taking sides with the revolutionary movement that had been started, and to get an American control of the government, which I did not approve of, for I considered it a dishonorable movement; but still, if I had landed, they being my countrymen, I might have got mixed up with them. They were conquered and all sentenced to death, and shot. It is barely possible I might have shared their fate. I have often thought since I made a good escape by not landing.

The course of the steamer is frequently in sight of land. The storms I have referred to were tropical storms, lasting but a short time. The ocean is generally very mild all the distance, three thousand five hundred miles from Panama to San Francisco. North of San Francisco the storms are somewhat similar to the Atlantic ocean storms. The passengers on the return trip were in the best of spirits; they were returning home; all of them had been more or less successful in California, and I can recall to my mind many pleasant times we had on board the steamship. The porpoise are very numerous on the Pacific ocean; there were often, for days, schools of them on the sides of the steamer, throwing themselves out of the water, and then diving in again; great numbers, at the same time, seeming like the motion of a revolving wheel. Occasionally we would hear the cry, "There she blows;" a jet of water being thrown up many feet high in the air—a sperm whale had come up to breathe. We frequently saw flying fish. One day there was a school of them landed on the steamer; they are similar to other fish, except having wings, but not of very large size. At another time a booby bird came on the steamer. It got its name from its stupidity. We frequently saw them on the water, floating on a piece of board or a stick of wood; sailors say they have seen them five hundred miles out to sea in that way. This is one you could take up and handle; it made no resistance. On the coast of Central America we saw two mountain peaks of great height, standing out, individually, like the Pyramids, said to be extinct volcanoes that were thrown up from the internal fires of the earth, and which, at one time, belched forth melted lava and fire.

We arrived safe in Panama. I was so near home that I thought I might as well return and see my friends, and take a fresh start for California, and try my fortune once more. They had commenced building the railroad over the Isthmus, but it was not completed, so we crossed over to Cruces, the head of navigation on the Chagres river, and went down that to its mouth, and there took the steamer *Georgia* for New York, commanded by Captain Porter, of the United States navy—the man who had control of the vessels in going down the Mississippi river and successfully passing Vicksburg, which had so much to do with its capture. He was a perfect gentleman, and commanded your admiration with the skill of his management of the vessel. There were on the vessel well-dressed pickpockets, who went from New York to the Isthmus, to return by the steamers to the city, for the chances of robbing the returning Californians of their gold dust, as all of them had more or less of it on their persons. One unfortunate victim of their wiles appealed strongly to my sympathies. He was an English sailor, and had been two or three years up in the gold mines, and had $3,000 or $4,000 in gold dust in a buckskin bag on his person. He showed it to me. I advised him to deposit it with the purser for safety; that I had done so with mine. He said they could not rob him. He was about the happiest man I ever saw. He was richer, in feeling, than the Vanderbilts. He said he had a wife and children in Liverpool, and would take the first steamer from New York to that port. He said he had not seen his family for several years, and now that he had gold he could make them all happy. He was in the steerage. A few days after I heard he was sick. He had fainted. Some parties had helped him up; evidently pickpockets had taken that opportunity to rob him; his gold was all gone. I explained his case to Captain Porter, but nothing could be done. There was no way to identify his gold dust from any other; it was all alike. When he arrived in New York, he would have to go to the hospital until he got well enough to ship on some other vessel for $14 per month, and not be able to return to his wife and children with his gold, and make them happy, while these black-hearted villains were spending his money, his hard earnings of years. I entered in a bond, with myself, that if I were ever on a jury I would never show any mercy to a thief.

As we were sailing along many ships and schooners came in sight. We were evidently nearing the great port of New York. The land of Staten Island soon came in sight covered with snow. It was late in the fall. It was the first I had seen since my departure from the same port, except on the highest peaks of the Sierra Nevada mountains. Here ends my personal adventures of the days of the Forty-niners, to be continued by the peroration on California.

PERORATION.

On my return, in looking over my finances, I was no poorer than when I left. It must be evident to the reader that I had acquired no wealth to astonish my friends with my riches, which was the visionary expectation of the early pioneers to the gold Eldorado. I have been writing from personal recollections of events that occurred forty-five years ago. Of course, there was nothing in my enterprises, or the little fluctuations of fortune that would be of particular interest to any one; but in the form of a personal narrative, it was the only way I could recall vividly to my mind, the events of so long ago. There were a series of articles published in the *Century* magazine two years ago, which I read with great interest, for they were truthful, but no book has ever been published that took in fully those two years when common labor was $16 per day, payable in gold. Such an event was never known to occur before, and probably never will again. I have not drawn on my imagination in the least in this narrative. I have simply attempted to portray from memory events that actually occurred under my own observation. Any Forty-niner will concede the truth of my narrative. I did not return to California as I had expected. Cupid's arrow pierced my heart in the person of a young lady, and sealed my fate. I had a cottage built in the quiet and beautiful valley of Schoharie, where I have passed more than thirty years of happy married life. While not possessing the wealth of the successful pioneer, I have been content.

THE NOTES

(1) The text is a little confusing. Actually, Knower sailed on July 1, 1849 on the steamer *Crescent City*. Although the *Crescent City* was later owned by the United States Mail Steamship Company, at this time it was owned by Charles Morgan and associates, and operated by J. Howard & Son. Supported by mail subsidies, the dominant carriers on the Panama route were the United States Mail Steamship Company on the Atlantic side, and the Pacific Mail Steamship Company on the Pacific, although there was always competition. The *Crescent City* continued in this trade until 1856 when it was lost on a reef in the Gulf of Mexico.

(2) Colonel B. was Colonel John J. Bryant who became one of San Francisco's best known professional gamblers, and a prominent citizen. He ran a combined hotel and gambling saloon, known as the Bryant House, formerly the Ward House; it was said that when the Colonel was behind the table all limits were off. As Knower later mentions, in May, 1850 Bryant was a candidate for sheriff of San Francisco, with the famous Colonel Jack C. Hays as his chief opponent. Bryant lost the election as well as a $10,000 bet on himself. The election was typical of the times with marching bands, dinners, and free drinks. Bryant lost the election not because of any bad odor that might have attached to him as a gambler, but because of the great personal popularity of Hays. Although not very active, Bryant was a member of the Committee of Vigilance of 1851.

(3) The United States Consul was William Nelson; in addition to Nelson, Elijah Payne and Amos B. Corwin also served in this capacity in Panama during 1849.

(4) There were several others among the *Crescent City's* passengers who were or would become prominent in California. Perhaps the most notable figure was Lieutenant Edward F. Beale who had come to California with Commodore Stockton and was an officer in his battalion, en route to the assistance of General S. W. Kearny at the time of the battle of San Pascual. Later he was the federally appointed superintendent of Indian affairs in California, and state Surveyor General. Beale also acquired large real estate holdings and became wealthy.

F. W. Macondray became one of San Francisco's most successful merchants; he was a city councilman in 1850, and was very active in the affairs of the Vigilance Committee of 1851. He can be called one of the civic leaders of his time.

James W. Mandeville located in Tuolumne County and was both an Assemblyman and Senator in the State Legislature. He held many other public offices and was State Controller at the time of his death in 1876.

Another passenger that had a lengthy political career was Philip A. Roach. Before coming to California he served in the United States Consulates at Havre and Lisbon. In California, Roach was the last Alcalde and first Mayor of Monterey; he held many other public offices including that of United States Customs Appraiser at San Francisco. After 1867, when he bought an interest in the San Francisco *Examiner,* most of his life was spent in journalism. In 1860–61 he was President of the Society of California Pioneers.

(5) Lieutenant M. proved to be impossible of identification. The only name in the *Crescent City* passenger list prefixed with "Lieutenant" was that of Beale. A good many of the Texas Rangers followed Colonel Jack Hays to California, and there was a John Moore who was an officer in the Rangers and a John Moore who was a passenger. In view of the rather daring conduct of Lieutenant M. and his selection as a lead man, there is a possibility that they were one and the same.

(6) Colonel P. would be Colonel Perez, who has been mentioned as one of the more reliable persons in the business of moving freight and persons across the Isthmus. Kemble, John Haskell, *The Panama Route, 1848–1869* (Berkeley and Los Angeles 1943) page 173. Professor Kemble's book is outstanding; the research involved was tremendous, and the work is both scholarly and readable. It is certainly the most important study of one of the principal approaches to California.

(7) Mr. Haight was Samuel W. Haight, who had come to California as a sutler with Stevenson's regiment. The Miners' Bank was founded by Dr. Steven A. Wright, with Haight and J. C. L. Wadsworth as partners, at the end of 1848. This was probably San Francisco's first bank in a strict sense of the word, although a

strong claim can be made for the banking firm of Naglee & Sinton which opened for business on January 9, 1849. At this time the words, "bank" and "banking" were used very loosely, and many express companies and larger mercantile firms performed what were essentially banking functions. In any event the Miners' Bank prospered and continued until 1855, the time of general bank failures in San Francisco. The Miners' Bank also, along with several others, operated as a private mint and issued gold coins. A reproduction of a ten dollar piece issued by this bank, stamped in gold, may be found in *New Varieties of Gold and Silver Coins, Counterfeit Coins and Bullion,* by Jacob R. Eckfeldt and William E. DuBois (Philadelphia, 1850). This interesting book when issued contained in a mica envelope two samples of California gold flakes; it is hardly necessary to remark that today few copies still have their gold.

(8) This delay on the Pacific side of the Isthmus was experienced by many who chose the Panama route. See Kemble *(supra)* pages 176–177 and Lewis, Oscar, *Sea Routes to the Gold Fields* (New York, 1949). One can still imagine the feelings provoked by this delay on the way to the land of gold. Great dissatisfaction was expressed as to the actions of Zachrisson, Nelson & Co., the agents for the Pacific Mail Steamship Company. On August 20 and 22 the Americans in Panama held meetings at the American Hotel to discuss their various grievances, and this was reported in the *Panama Star* for the 25th; in part it said:

"But the great cause of complaint was the conduct of Messrs. Zachrisson, Nelson & Co., who have transacted the business of Messrs. Howland and Aspinwall in such a manner as to convince all (we know of no exception), that their object is not to advance the interests of the Pacific Company, but to promote their own private interests to the detriment of the Company, and great injustice to Americans. No other reason can be imagined why they should insult American citizens as they have done. Gentlemen who at home are highly respected, have gone to the office, and in view of the dangers of remaining in this place, have asked Messrs. Z. N. & Co. in a respectful manner, "When do you think the *Oregon* will sail?" They have insultingly replied, "She will sail when she starts!" . . . . Do they give you any previous notice? No! Do they recognize any priority of claim? No! There are passengers here who were here when the *Panama* sailed a month ago. Do the agents tell them to register their names? No! No priority is recognized—passengers of the *M. C. Draper* just arrived, get tickets, while those who have remained here a month or two get none.

No advertisement is issued telling people they may register their names, with the hope of getting tickets—and if one's name is registered, it is altered from its place on the list to suit the whim of the agents, or more likely their interests.

The Public, however have taken the matter in hand now, and here we drop it for the present." (Reprinted in the *Quarterly* of the Society of California Pioneers, Vol. VI, No. 1, March 1929.)

(9) A good many of the early travelers tended to exaggerate the unhealthiness of the Panama climate. Probably some of the illness was caused by the exertion of the crossing, and intemperance in eating and drinking. In any event, there were rather severe epidemics of cholera in 1849 and 1850.

(10) The Panama was a wooden side-wheel steamer built especially for the Pacific Mail Steamship Company, and first sailed from New York for San Francisco on February 15, 1849. It was in the Panama-to-San Francisco run for several years, and later was sold to the Mexican government and rechristened *Juarez*.

(11) In the absence of a cholera epidemic, Acapulco authorities welcomed American vessels and it was a regular port of call on both the northern and southern passages.

(12) It has been impossible to place Mr. G. with any degree of certainty. He may have been A. H. Guild, an Englishman, who was a partner in the active commercial firm of Grayson, Guild & Co. Andrew J. Grayson of this firm was a particularly interesting person. In 1851 he went to San Jose and became a competent, self-trained ornithologist and drew some remarkable bird pictures; he has been called. "The Audubon of the Pacific".

Knower is in error when he lists David S. Terry as a fellow passenger. Terry arrived in San Francisco in September, 1849 after an overland trip from Texas by way of New Mexico and Arizona. A. E. Wagstaff, *Life of David S. Terry*, (San Francisco, 1892) page 52; Buchanan A. Russell, *David S. Terry of California—Dueling*

Judge, (San Marino, 1956) pages 7 and 8. The reference to Terry's death is a little simplistic; however, the matter is covered in both of the biographies cited above and in the general histories of California. Here it is sufficient to say that he led an eventful and dramatic life in California.

(13) The dates of the discovery of San Francisco bay, and the entry by the *San Carlos* are October 30, 1769 and August 5, 1775, according to the most recent studies. Treutlein, Theodore E., *San Francisco Bay—Discovery and Colonization, 1769–1776,* (San Francisco, 1968) pages 16 and 65. Construction of the Mission began in April 1782, and it was founded by the Franciscan Fathers; the Jesuits were never in what is today the state of California. Berger, John A., *The Franciscan Missions of California.* (New York, 1941) pages 83, 341.

(14) There are some minor variations in the dates given. For example the date generally accepted for the gold discovery is January 24, 1848. As this book indicates, Colonel Jonathan D. Stevenson remained in California and was a prominent and successful businessman. The best report of Stevenson's regiment is found in *California Expedition—Stevenson's Regiment of First New York Volunteers,* by Guy J. Giffen, (Oakland, 1951).

(15) Sutter acquired his Sacramento property under a Mexican grant, and purchased the Russian property at Fort Ross which he was to pay for largely in the delivery of grain.

(16) Wilson Shannon was Governor of Ohio in 1838, and was Minister to Mexico in 1844-45. He spent about eighteen months in California.

(17) Samuel Brannan was never in Stevenson's regiment and arrived in San Francisco on the *Brooklyn* from New York in August 1846 with a group of Mormons. He was for many years a man of prominence and influence in San Francisco and Sacramento. As Knower indicates, he made several fortunes but died a poor man. There are two biographies of Brannan: Bailey, Paul, *Sam Brannan and the California Mormons,* (Los Angeles, 1943); Scott, Reva, *Samuel Brannan and the Golden Fleece,* (New York, 1944). The reader should be warned that in the latter the author "puts words in the characters' mouths."

(18) It has been estimated that between 1,300 and 1,500 doctors arrived in California during the gold rush. Harris, Henry, M.D., *California Medical Story,* (Springfield, Illinois: Baltimore Maryland, 1932) page 74.

(19) The callous treatment of the California Indians by some of the forty-niners was an ugly feature of the gold rush. In the minds of some the Indian was simply an animal that could be shot at sight. Many annals of the time mention the needless slaughter of Indians. For a more civilized view see, Browne, J. Ross, *Crusoe's Island,* (New York, 1864) pages 303 and 304.

(20) Most estimates were lower than this.

(21) The *Senator* was perhaps the best known of the steamers that ran between San Francisco and Sacramento. The *Senator* replaced an earlier steamer the *Mint* which made its first run in October 1849; also in October the *McKim* was placed in this service.

(22) Happy Valley was roughly the area now bounded by Mission, First, Natoma, and Second streets. One traveler found the Valley not very happy: "The ground was of course, low, damp, and muddy; and the most unmistakable evidence of discomfort, misery, and sickness, met our view on every side, for the locality was one of the unwholesomest in the vicinity of the town." Ryan, William Redmond, *Personal Adventures in Upper and Lower California in 1848–9,* (London, 1850) volume II, page 271.

Today there is a bar with the same name in the Sheraton-Palace Hotel which is neither damp nor muddy.

(23) The telegraph was on Telegraph Hill; Rincon Point was a projection into the bay somewhat to the south.

(24) Port collector James Collier, after an arduous overland trip, arrived in San Francisco in November 1849, and served until January 1851. When Collier left office it was alleged that he was short in his accounts to the extent of $391,364.25, and the government filed suit against him and his bondsmen in this amount. Collier filed a counterclaim and the final judgment was in his favor in the amount of $8,110. There is an interesting book on Collier: Foreman, Grant, *The Adventures of James Collier,* (Chicago, 1937).

(25) The effort to identify Mr. R. proved to be most frustrating. There were several possibilities, each one finally rejected. Curiously,

one candidate, Charles C. Ross, a prominent capitalist and merchant, had one of the attributes later assigned by Knower to Mr. G; the first post office was in the "New York Store" of Ross.

(26) Colonel Stevenson died on February 14, 1894.

(27) The Hounds incident occurred in the latter part of July, 1849 and thus before Knower's arrival. A hoodlum element had developed and in this month about twenty men were arrested and tried before a special court consisting of acting Alcalde T. M. Leavenworth, William M. Gwin, and James C. Ward. A good many were found guilty and the punishment generally was banishment. See Hittell, Theodore H., *History of California* (San Francisco, 1897) Volume II, pages 725–727.

(28) L. was T. M. Leavenworth, an Episcopal minister and doctor of medicine who was appointed Alcalde by Colonel R. B. Mason, and served from September 1848 to August 1849. He was unpopular, but in the main this stemmed from the fact that he was part of the military government controlled by the military governor, at a time when the citizens of San Francisco desired to govern themselves. There was a running quarrel between the military governor and those who were endeavoring to create local government. See Williams, Mary Floyd, *History of San Francisco Committee of Vigilance of 1851,* (Berkeley, 1921) pages 98–101. There appears to be no justification for "seems to have been the butt of the boys", and, of course, Leavenworth was never elected Alcalde. Incidentally the book by Mary Floyd Williams is an outstanding and valuable work; although the Committee of Vigilance is treated in depth, this is also an excellent history of early San Francisco.

(29) Knower's general thinking is correct, but he is in error as to the details. There was no uniform price of $16; improvement was not essential, and the usual lot size was fifty varas.. Until 1851 the government of San Francisco was in the main financed by the sale of lots both on petition and at auction. There were many legal questions which were not clear at the time and this led to arguments as to validity of titles. The best work in this area is still, Wheeler, Alfred, *Land Titles in San Francisco and the Laws Affecting the Same,* (San Francisco, 1852). There is also a valuable summary in Robinson, W. W., *Land in California,* (Berkeley and Los Angeles, 1948)

pages 232–235. As to the land question as a whole this book has been called a classic.

(30) The events to honor the late President Zachary Taylor took place on August 29, 1850, and constituted San Francisco's first great civic demonstration. There were orations and the procession was huge; in the latter nearly every organization in the city was represented. Those who left memoirs of this time all comment on this civic outpouring, and most mention the Chinese who marched as a group.

(31) See note 2. Another source states that Colonel Bryant spent $50,000 in his campaign.

(32) This would be the Ward House and it was expensive. Rooms were $250 a month and as indicated, meals were costly. Bancroft, Hubert Howe, *History of California,* (San Francisco, 1890) Volume VI, pages 190–191.

(33) San Franciscans were notably generous as to charities; however, the incident involving Mr. W. could not be verified.

(34) When David C. Broderick first came to California, he and Frederick D. Kohler started a minting and assay office and issued gold slugs and coins. Kohler was the technician and Broderick was the business manager.

(35) I would say in the fall; the convention opened on September 1, 1849, and closed on October 13th.

(36) One authority has stated, "There are, excluding the article on the boundary, one hundred and thirty-six sections in the California constitution. Of these about seventy are taken from the constitution of Iowa and about twenty from that of New York". Goodwin, Cardinal, *The Establishment of State Government in California,* (New York, 1941) page 242.

(37) This is basically correct. The conflict between Broderick and William M. Gwin is a fascinating tale of political machinations. Broderick had supported Gwin on the understanding that Federal patronage would be controlled by the former. Partially because President Buchanan was very friendly with Gwin, it did not work out that way. See Williams, David A., *David C. Broderick—A Political Portrait,* (San Marino, 1969) chapter 9.

(38) Knower was right; one historian said, "Lumber was worth four

hundred dollars a thousand feet in the fall of 1849, twelve times the present price, and in the spring of 1850 it would not sell for enough to pay freight." Hittell, John S., *A History of the City of San Francisco*, (San Francisco, 1878) page 212.

(39) There is a little confusion here. The first banking house to fail was that of Naglee & Sinton in September 1850; however Henry M. Naglee a little later paid all claims in full. The initial "W" suggests Wells & Co., a banking firm organized by Thomas G. Wells. This firm started in the early part of 1850, was extremely profitable at first and then got into difficulty; however it did not close until 1851, after Knower's departure. In any event, Wells did not shoot himself. See Cross, Ira B., *Financing an Empire—History of Banking in California*, (Chicago—San Francisco—Los Angeles, 1927) pages 48, 52, and 57.

(40) Henry Meiggs, or "Honest Harry" as he was called, was a most prominent and well-liked business man of the time. He constructed Meiggs' wharf and was an alderman during three administrations. However he forged city warrants and borrowed on them. When these notes became due he would reborrow on more forged warrants. Obviously there would come a time when this would have to end. This occurred in October, 1854 when he lavishly fitted out a vessel and he and his family sailed for Chile never to return, leaving debts in the approximate amount of $1,000,000. In Chile and Peru he did make a fortune as a railway contractor. This was one of San Francisco's greatest scandals.

(41) As already noted (see note 29) there were various difficulties with land titles in San Francisco. In the first place there was a question as to whether the municipality was entitled to four square leagues of land as an original Mexican pueblo. To establish this, the city filed a suit against the United States (which would have title in the event this was not vested in the city). John W. Dwinelle represented the city and this led to his famous book, *The Colonial History of San Francisco*, (San Francisco, 1863). There were later expanded editions. San Francisco prevailed in this litigation. In the latter part of 1849 G. Q. Colton was Justice of the Peace and undertook to make grants of city lots. As to this, the Town Council on December 21, 1849 adopted the following resolution:

"Whereas, it had this day been made to appear to the Ayuntamiento that G. Q. Colton, a Justice of the Peace in and for the town of San Francisco, has assumed the authority and pretends to exercise the right of selling, granting and disposing of lots within the limits of said town,

"Resolved, that Archibald C. Peachy, Esq., City Attorney, be directed to institute legal proceedings against the said Colton to restrain him in such illegal and unwarrantable practices, and to make him amenable by due process of law for a misdemeanor and malfeasance in office." (Wheeler, *(supra)* page 20.

Eventually the Colton grants were held to be invalid. The title questions were also clouded by squatterism, but this did not reach the magnitude in San Francisco that it did in other areas, notably Sacramento and Oakland.

(42) As already mentioned (note 13) the California missions were established by the Franciscan order. There were twenty-one.

(43) Although Knower never realized anything from it, Tuolumne City did come into a short existance and is shown on several early maps, for example, the map of C. D. Gibbes (1852) in Holmes, Evelyn H., *The Southern Mines of California,* (San Francisco, 1930). As mentioned, the location was too far south to be the head of navigation and the town withered away.

(44) During 1849 to 1851 San Francisco was to suffer several disastrous fires; the principal ones were on December 24, 1849, May 4, 1850, June 14, 1850, September 17, 1850, May 4, 1851, and June 22, 1851.

(45) This would appear to be a different G., and was probably G. W. Goss who maintained an exchange office in the Parker House facing the Plaza. Mr. Goss may have been ruined, but in the usual case, after a fire any gold on the premises could be recovered.

(46) See notes 13 and 22. The Mission was about three miles west of Happy Valley.

(47) Probably what Mr. R. had started was taken over by another. In 1850 there was a brewery known as the Empire Brewery located in Happy Valley operated by W. Ball, sometimes spelled Bull. It has been said that this was the first of its kind. Bancroft, *supra,* Volume VI, page 181. On the other hand, John Henry Brown states

that the first brewery was started by Francis G. Owen at Pacific and Dupont streets. Brown, John Henry, *Reminiscences and Incidents of Early Days in San Francisco 1845–50,* (San Francisco, 1933) page 101. This is a reprint of the first edition of 1886.

(48) Several experimented with diving equipment of one kind or another, but without success. This was an example of various kinds of apparatus, the promotion of which was better than the performance. Hittell, Theodore H., *supra* Volume III, page 60.

(49) One has the feeling that creditors were not far behind.

(50) The *Ecuador* was a side-wheel steamer owned by an English firm, the Pacific Steam Navigation Company, and operated on the west coast of South America. It made but one trip to San Francisco in July, 1850, returning in September, which fixes the time of Knower's departure. Even though Knower may exaggerate, it was certainly a mismanaged voyage.

COLOPHON

THE ILLUSTRATIONS of 'forty-niner "types" in this book were reproduced from originals drawn by Augusto (in some references "Auguste") Ferran. The creator of "The Jenny Lind Theatre" (*circa* 1850, on Portsmouth Square), was regrettably unidentifiable. The "Bill for Room and Board" was found in Knower's original edition, and the Map of San Francisco is from the publisher's collection.

The text pages of this book were composed at San Francisco in Linotype Times Roman types at The Filmer Brothers Press–Taylor & Taylor, who also performed the printing and binding. The illustrations, except for the map, were lithographed at Ashland, Oregon, at The Inland Press. The papers are Curtis Utopian Text and Warren's Lustro Enamel, and the binding is in Columbia Mills' natural Bolton buckram.

The volume was designed by Lewis Osborne.